the Picky Palate cookbook

Jenny Flake

Photography by Matt Armendariz

WILEY

John Wiley & Sons, Inc.

Published simultaneously in Canada

No part of this publication may be reproduced, stored in a retrieval system, or transmitted in any form or by any means, electronic, mechanical, photocopying, recording, scanning, or otherwise, except as permitted under Section 107 or 108 of the 1976 United States Copyright Act, without either the prior written permission of the Publisher, or authorization through payment of the appropriate per-copy fee to the Copyright Clearance Center, 222 Rosewood Drive, Danvers, MA 01923, (978) 750-8400, fax (978) 646-8600, or on the web at www.copyright.com. Requests to the Publisher for permission should be addressed to the Permissions Department, John Wiley & Sons, Inc., 111 River Street, Hoboken, NJ 07030, (201) 748-6011, fax (201) 748-6008, or online at http://www.wiley.com/go/permissions.

Limit of Liability/Disclaimer of Warranty: While the publisher and the author have used their best efforts in preparing this book, they make no representations or warranties with respect to the accuracy or completeness of the contents of this book and specifically disclaim any implied warranties of merchantability or fitness for a particular purpose. No warranty may be created or extended by sales representatives or written sales materials. The advice and strategies contained herein may not be suitable for your situation. You should consult with a professional where appropriate. Neither the publisher nor the author shall be liable for any loss of profit or any other commercial damages, including but not limited to special, incidental, consequential, or other damages.

For general information about our other products and services, please contact our Customer Care Department within the United States at (800) 762-2974, outside the United States at (317) 572-3993 or fax (317) 572-4002.

Wiley publishes in a variety of print and electronic formats and by print-on-demand. Some material included with standard print versions of this book may not be included in e-books or in print-on-demand. If this book refers to media such as a CD or DVD that is not included in the version you purchased, you may download this material at http://booksupport.wiley.com. For more information about Wiley products, visit www.wiley.com.

Library of Congress Cataloging-in-Publication Data

Flake, Jenny, 1976-

The picky palate cookbook / Jenny Flake ; photography by Matt Armendariz.

    p. cm.

Includes index.

ISBN 978-1-118-09512-6 (cloth); 978-1-118-37146-6 (ebk.);

978-1-118-37147-3 (ebk.); 978-1-118-37150-3 (ebk.)

1. Quick and easy cooking. 2. Cookbooks. I. Title.

TX833.5.F64 2012

641.5'55--dc23

                            2011037512

Printed in China

10 9 8 7 6 5 4 3 2 1

Contents

Introduction

Had No Idea I'd Become Such a Foodie!

I will never forget standing in my brand-new kitchen late 2001 in Gilbert, Arizona, with my husband. We had been married for four years and were so excited to be in our first new home. I remember looking around, admiring my shiny new appliances and clean cabinets, when all of a sudden a feeling of panic came over me: I realized . . . I don't know how to cook anything! OK, maybe a grilled cheese and a can of tomato soup, but that was it. It was actually a horrible feeling. With the New Year just around the corner, I made it a serious goal to teach myself everything I could about cooking.

I was not messing around; I bought dozens of cookbooks, read them like novels, and watched Food Network religiously. Recipes and flavor combinations were intriguing to me. I was like a little sponge soaking up everything culinary. Tyler Florence, Paula Deen, and Ina Garten became household names. Cooking was becoming a true joy in my life, and I was even playing around with creating my own recipes. Amidst all of my cooking, I was also working as a dental hygienist and had our first son in the summer of 2002. Life was great.

One late night, I was watching Food Network as usual and saw this exciting commercial for the Pillsbury Bake-Off. They talked all about home cooks who would compete for a million dollars. I was intrigued, to say the least. The thought of creating recipes and possibly winning money for it sounded like fun to me. I jumped off of the couch, ran over to my computer as the rest of the family slept, and researched all about this cooking competition. Over the next couple of months I had a blast creating my own recipes that I entered into the Bake-Off. I entered dozens of recipes in hopes that one of them would get me into the contest. The deadline passed, and five or six months went by. I was still cooking, working, and enjoying being a new mom. I'll never forget the night I got the phone call that, little did I know, would change everything.

A very nice woman on the other end of the line informed me that my Taco Ranch Chicken Sandwiches had made it as one of the 100 recipes and would take me to the 2004 Pillsbury Bake-Off in Hollywood. I was speechless and could hardly believe I really made it! All of my hard work playing around in the kitchen had actually paid off.

To make a very long story short, I did not win the million-dollar prize that year but had the time of my life competing and meeting wonderful people. I continued a journey of competitive cooking for three-and-a-half years, which are some of my favorite memories. My little family traveled all over the country, and I was even on Food Network a few times when I competed on *The*

Ultimate Recipe Showdown and *Build a Better Burger Competition*. Some of my best wins were from my Coconut Macadamia Shrimp with Warm Tropical Salsa that won $10,000 in the Southern Living Contest and my Chicken Taco Cornbread Wedges with Ranchero Cilantro Drizzle that won $5,000 in the National Cornbread Cook-Off. Such fun times we had.

After I had been competing for three years, my boys were getting older, and I just knew it was time to take a break from competition, but that didn't mean I stopped cooking. I remember one late night chatting with my sister on the phone talking about this thing called "blogging" that was popping up all over the web. She started a family blog and I loved the idea. It wasn't long before I figured out I should start a blog where I could share the recipes I loved creating. I thought "Picky Palate" was a catchy and fitting title for my blog, since my young family is definitely composed of finicky eaters. In October 2007, Picky Palate was born, and what a journey it has been.

In 2010, I decided that I would make Picky Palate not only my hobby, but my business. It was the best decision I could have made, because now I get to create recipes for busy families for a living and I could not be happier. Picky Palate has become my passion and I couldn't ask for a more perfect job. I get to create recipes, capture food photography, and share it with those who read my blog; I truly love it.

I have learned a thing or two about feeding little picky eaters. Here are some of my favorite tips.

Slowly introduce new foods to your little ones. Don't expect them to jump up and down with excitement the first or even second time you give them a new food. Persistence and patience are the key.

Make your vegetables and fruit that your little ones may not be very excited about into fun shapes. Use small cookie cutters and cut their fruits and veggies into something new and exciting. Play "What can we make out of our food?" Chances are they'll love it.

Have your kids in the kitchen with you while preparing meals. When they have a hand in dinner, they'll be proud of what they've done and want to eat it.

Don't make more than one dinner per night for your family. Some moms I know make dinner for each child because they don't like what was fixed. No way! Try a "No, Thank You" policy. If your child doesn't like what was made for dinner, simply have them try at least one bite each time, then say "No, thank you" if they don't like it. Even if they don't like it the first time, chances are they'll eventually learn to enjoy it. If they know there is only one choice for dinner, they won't want to be hungry later.

Make dinner a fun experience, where the kids are excited to sit down. Your vibe will rub off on them. When they see their parents oohing and aahing over what they are eating, they'll be more likely to eventually join you. You can even play games with your food while you are eating, like "Let's see who can take more bites," or "How many different colors of the rainbow can we eat off our plate?" Something with a little competition can be fun.

Try naming your child's food something fun and playful: Sammy's Saucy Superhero Spaghetti, Luke's Green Giant Broccoli, Anna's Princess Smile Oranges . . . . You get the idea—make it fun.

Purchase inexpensive "fun" kids plates that might be exciting to your child. If they are eating off of their favorite superhero or character, they will want to gobble up their food.

Incorporate a healthy smoothie night. Have some yogurt and lots of fresh fruit on hand. Have your child help put everything in the blender and watch it turn into a beautiful healthy treat!

Avoid too many snacks before dinnertime; keep them hungry for their last meal of the day.

Most importantly, be patient and make mealtime fun. Persistence will be your best friend

As a busy mom and food blogger, I have learned how important it is to keep a well-stocked kitchen to save time when preparing meals. I put together a list of my "must-haves" to get me through busy weekdays with no stress. I recommend going through your pantry and tossing out the old items and getting things organized. You will feel so much better. Before you know it, you'll have a well-stocked kitchen you can cook from any night of the week.

Pantry Must-Haves

- An assortment of canned beans: black beans, white beans, refried beans, pinto beans, chickpeas (garbanzo beans), and a variety of dried beans
- Canned diced tomatoes, crushed tomatoes, tomato sauce, tomato paste, and a good BBQ sauce
- Canned tuna and canned chunk chicken
- An assortment of rice, quinoa, couscous, and dried pasta
- Panko Japanese bread crumbs and traditional bread crumbs
- Chicken broth
- Jars of your favorite salsas
- Peanut butter, jams, and jellies
- An assortment of crackers
- Honey and maple syrup
- A variety of breakfast cereals
- Olive oil, vegetable oil, canola oil
- Balsamic vinegar, rice wine vinegar, apple cider vinegar
- Seasonings and spices: kosher salt, sea salt, black peppercorns, ground cumin, chili powder, garlic salt, garlic powder, smoked paprika, cayenne pepper, Italian seasoning, basil, thyme, rosemary, cinnamon, vanilla beans, and pure vanilla extract
- All-purpose flour, oatmeal, granulated sugar, brown sugar, powdered sugar, baking soda, baking powder, cornstarch, cream of tartar
- An assortment of chocolate chips, nuts, marshmallows, brownie mixes, cake mixes, and frostings

Refrigerator Must-Haves

- Milk, buttermilk, heavy cream
- Eggs
- Unsalted butter
- Spreadable butter
- An assortment of cheeses: cream cheese, Parmesan cheese, cheddar cheese, mozzarella cheese, feta cheese, and Gorgonzola cheese
- An assortment of yogurts
- Yellow mustard, brown mustard, ketchup, Worcestershire sauce, hot sauce, and salad dressing
- Bacon
- Carrots, celery, onions, garlic, broccoli, sweet peppers, avocados
- Salad greens, parsley, cilantro, and fresh herbs
- Apples, oranges, kiwis, lemons, and limes

Freezer Must-Haves

- Chicken breast
- Ground beef
- Shrimp
- Sausage
- Bread (I keep loaves on hand for sandwiches and garlic toast)
- Pizza dough
- Pita bread (makes a quick pizza crust when you need a quick dinner)
- Pie crust
- Puff pastry
- Cookie dough
- Bags of frozen vegetables

Chapter 1

Rise and Shine

Recipes That Will Perk Up Breakfast and Brunch

I love seeing Nutella all over my boys' faces when we enjoy this over-the-top breakfast. Nutella is one of those spreads that is good enough to eat right out of the jar, but wait until you try it stuffed in my French toast along with bananas. Serve warm, dusted with powdered sugar, and/or drizzled with maple syrup, with a bowl of fresh fruit.

Nutella-Banana-Stuffed French Toast

4   large eggs

½   cup milk

2   tablespoons packed light brown sugar

1   tablespoon vanilla extract

6   slices bread

3   tablespoons Nutella

2   medium bananas, sliced ⅛-inch thick

    Powdered sugar, for serving

    Pure maple syrup, for serving

1. Heat a large skillet over medium heat and spray with nonstick cooking spray.

2. Add the eggs, milk, brown sugar, and vanilla to a large bowl and whisk to combine. In batches, dip the bread in the egg mixture and add to the skillet. Cook until browned, 2 to 3 minutes, then cook on the other side for 2 to 3 minutes more. Transfer to a serving plate. Spread 1 tablespoon Nutella each on 3 toasts, then top with the banana slices. Top with the remaining 3 toasts, cut in half on a diagonal, and serve warm with the powdered sugar and maple syrup.

Makes
6
Servings

There's nothing like an impressive breakfast that only takes two minutes to get into the oven. Serving breakfast in individual ramekins is such a treat. The kids enjoy having their own special little dish to enjoy. Experiment with different toppings such as bacon, breakfast sausage, peppers, and onions. They make great additions. Prepare yourself for flavor-packed eggs that are perfect with buttered toast and a tall glass of orange juice.

Pesto-Parmesan Baked Eggs

¼	cup prepared pesto
8	large eggs
½	teaspoon kosher salt
¼	teaspoon freshly ground black pepper
4	teaspoons freshly grated Parmesan cheese

1. Preheat the oven to 425°F and spray four 2-cup ramekins with nonstick cooking spray.

2. Spread 1 tablespoon of the pesto inside the bottom of each ramekin. Crack 2 eggs into each ramekin, season with the salt and pepper, then top with the Parmesan cheese. Bake about 12 minutes, until the eggs are set, and serve warm.

Makes
4
Servings

You know when you are eating a big breakfast and take bites of pancake with bites of bacon and it's the best combination ever? Well, this simple morning muffin has that same effect with sweet and salty flavors throughout. Spread the maple butter on the inside of each muffin. Serve warm alongside your favorite breakfast with a cold glass of milk.

Maple-Bacon Muffins with Sweet Butter

2	large eggs
⅔	cup plus 2 tablespoons maple syrup
½	cup vegetable oil
¼	cup heavy cream
¼	cup sour cream
2	cups all-purpose flour
2	tablespoons granulated sugar
1	tablespoon baking powder
½	teaspoon kosher salt
½	pound sliced bacon, cooked until crisp and crumbled (about 1 cup)
4	tablespoons (½ stick) unsalted butter, softened

1. Preheat the oven to 400°F. Line a 12-count muffin pan with paper liners.

2. Add the eggs, ⅔ cup of the maple syrup, the vegetable oil, heavy cream, and sour cream to a large bowl and whisk to combine. Add the flour, sugar, baking powder, and salt to the wet ingredients and stir to combine. Add the bacon and stir to combine.

3. Fill the muffin cups ¾ full with batter. Bake for 15 to 18 minutes, or until a toothpick comes out clean from the center.

4. Add the butter and the remaining 2 tablespoons maple syrup to a small bowl and stir until well combined. Cut the muffins in half and spread with the maple butter. Serve warm.

Makes
12
Muffins

Having an omelet for breakfast is such a treat. The beauty of omelets is that you can get creative and experiment with what you have in your refrigerator. Have the kids sit at the counter and stir in their favorite ingredients. I gently press cooked hash browns in the bottom of ramekin dishes to form a crust, then layer bacon, eggs and cheese as the filling. Watch the eggs puff and turn light golden brown as they bake in the oven. Enjoy your individual omelet with a glass of orange juice and a bowl of fresh fruit.

Baked Hash Brown, Bacon, and Cheddar Omelets

1	tablespoon extra-virgin olive oil
2	cups frozen shredded hash browns, thawed
½	pound sliced bacon, cooked until crisp and crumbled (about 1 cup)
8	large eggs
2	tablespoons milk
¼	teaspoon kosher salt
¼	teaspoon freshly ground black pepper
½	cup shredded cheddar cheese
¼	cup chopped fresh parsley

1. Preheat the oven to 400°F. Spray four 2-cup ramekins with nonstick cooking spray.

2. Heat the olive oil in a large skillet over medium heat. Add the hash browns and cook, stirring, until browned, 5 to 8 minutes. Add ½ cup of the hash browns into the bottom of each ramekin. Top each with ¼ cup each of the bacon.

3. Add the eggs, milk, salt, and pepper to a large bowl and whisk to combine. Divide evenly among the ramekins. Top each with 2 tablespoons of the shredded cheddar cheese and 1 tablespoon of the parsley. Bake for 15 to 20 minutes, until the eggs are set.

Makes
4
Servings

I have had my fair share of breakfast casseroles over the years and thought it was about time I developed the ultimate recipe with all of my favorite ingredients. I use cut-up English muffins as the base; however, you can also use French bread or sourdough as a substitute. With so many great layers, have the kids take turns helping put the recipe together. Save yourself some time and prepare this casserole the night before, cover, refrigerate (up to 24 hours in advance), and pop in the oven the morning you need it.

English Muffin Breakfast Casserole Supreme

1	12.5-ounce package English muffins (6 count)
1	pound bulk breakfast sausage
2	tablespoons extra-virgin olive oil
½	cup finely chopped white onion
2	cups frozen shredded hash browns, thawed
12	large eggs
1	cup milk
½	teaspoon kosher salt
½	teaspoon freshly ground black pepper
⅛	teaspoon garlic salt
½	cup prepared mild salsa
1½	cups shredded cheddar cheese

1. Preheat the oven to 350°F and spray a 9×13-inch baking dish and a 12-inch skillet with nonstick cooking spray.

2. Tear or cut the English muffins into 1-inch pieces and line the bottom of the prepared baking dish.

3. Heat the prepared skillet over medium heat. Add the sausage and cook, breaking up the meat, until browned, 7 to 10 minutes. Transfer to a paper towel–lined plate and wipe the skillet clean.

4. Place the skillet back over medium heat and add the olive oil. Add the onion and cook, stirring, until tender, about 5 minutes. Add the hash browns and cook until browned, about 5 minutes. Remove from the heat.

5. Add the eggs, milk, salt, pepper, and garlic salt to a large bowl, whisking until well combined.

6. Layer the sausage evenly over the English muffins, then the hash browns and salsa. Pour the eggs on top and sprinkle with the cheddar cheese. Bake for 40 to 50 minutes, until the eggs are set. Serve warm.

Makes 8–10 Servings

This apple puff pancake has relaxing Saturday mornings in pajamas written all over it. I look forward to mornings like this when the boys hop up to the counter, help stir the batter, and watch the oven patiently as the pancake magically rises. If your family enjoys nuts, add ¼ cup of your favorite chopped nuts to the batter. The caramel syrup drizzled over the top is downright sinful but completely necessary. Serve with a bowl of fresh fruit.

Apple-Spice Puff Pancake with Caramel Syrup

9	tablespoons unsalted butter, divided
1	cup plus 1 tablespoon packed light brown sugar
1	cup peeled and chopped Granny Smith apple
½	teaspoon ground cinnamon
1	cup all-purpose flour
⅓	cup granulated sugar
¼	teaspoon plus ⅛ teaspoon kosher salt
5	large eggs
⅓	cup milk
1	teaspoon vanilla extract
¼	cup heavy cream
¼	cup sour cream

1. Preheat the oven to 425°F.

2. Melt 1 tablespoon of the butter and 1 tablespoon of the brown sugar in a 10-inch skillet over medium heat. Add the apple and cinnamon and cook, stirring, for 5 minutes. Remove from the heat.

3. Add the flour, sugar, and ⅛ teaspoon of the salt into a medium bowl, stirring to combine. Add the eggs, milk, and vanilla into a separate medium bowl, whisking to combine. Stir into the dry ingredients until well combined. Add the apples, stirring to combine.

4. Melt 4 tablespoons of the remaining butter in a 12-inch skillet over medium heat. Pour the pancake batter into the skillet. Bake for 18 to 22 minutes, until puffed and golden.

5. While the pancake is baking, melt the remaining 1 cup brown sugar, the remaining ¼ teaspoon salt, and 2 tablespoons of water in a small saucepan over medium heat. Cook, stirring, until bubbly and smooth, about 5 minutes. Add the remaining 4 tablespoons butter and stir until melted. Add the heavy cream and sour cream, stirring until well combined. Reduce the heat to low until ready to serve. Cut the puffed pancake into 4 wedges and drizzle each wedge with caramel syrup.

Makes **4** Servings

French toast happens on a very regular basis at our home, so I developed this aromatic streusel topping that gets baked right on top of the French toast. Bits of cinnamon and butter form a crust on top that's downright sinful. The kids are all smiles when you place this delightful meal in front of them. Enjoy drizzled with maple syrup and a side of fresh fruit.

Streusel Baked French Toast

1	12.5-ounce French baguette
8	large eggs
1	cup milk
¾	cup heavy cream
¾	cup packed light brown sugar, divided
1	tablespoon vanilla extract
½	teaspoon ground cinnamon
½	teaspoon kosher salt, divided
¼	cup all-purpose flour
4	tablespoons (½ stick) unsalted butter, cold
½	teaspoon ground cinnamon
	Maple syrup

1. Preheat the oven to 350°F and spray a 9×13-inch baking dish with nonstick cooking spray.

2. Cut the baguette into ½-inch slices and layer in the prepared baking dish. Add the eggs, milk, heavy cream, ¼ cup of the brown sugar, the vanilla, cinnamon, and ¼ teaspoon of the salt to a large bowl, whisking to combine. Pour over the bread.

3. Add the remaining ½ cup brown sugar, the flour, butter, cinnamon, and the remaining ¼ teaspoon salt to a medium bowl. With a fork or pastry cutter, cut the butter into the dry ingredients until the butter is combined with the flour and the mixture resembles small peas. Sprinkle evenly over the bread. Bake for 40 to 45 minutes, until the eggs are set. Let cool for 5 minutes before serving. Serve drizzled with maple syrup.

Makes **8** Servings

There is something so tempting about warm, savory quiche that makes for a perfect breakfast. I'm not sure if it's the buttery pie crust, the savory egg filling, or a combination of both that I like best. I developed this simple recipe that is full of vegetables, cheese, and lots of bacon. My father-in-law once said that you know you are eating good quiche if you don't need ketchup or hot sauce. I get a good laugh at that, and I must say you won't need either with this one.

Bacon and Cheddar Florentine Quiche

½ pound bacon, chopped

2 cups chopped fresh spinach leaves

½ cup finely chopped white onion

1 refrigerated 9-inch pie crust

8 large eggs

¼ cup milk

¼ teaspoon kosher salt

¼ teaspoon freshly ground black pepper

½ cup shredded cheddar cheese

2 tablespoons chopped fresh parsley

1. Preheat the oven to 350°F and spray a 9-inch pie plate with nonstick cooking spray.

2. Heat a large skillet over medium heat and cook the bacon, stirring until browned, about 10 minutes. Transfer the bacon to a paper towel–lined plate and discard all but 2 tablespoons of the drippings. Heat the reserved drippings over medium heat. Add the spinach and onion and cook, stirring, until the onions are tender and the spinach is wilted, about 5 minutes. Remove from the heat.

3. Unroll the pie crust and lay it at the bottom and up the sides of the prepared pie plate. With a fork, poke holes in the bottom, and partially bake the crust for 10 minutes. Remove from the oven.

4. Add the eggs, milk, salt, and pepper to a large bowl and whisk to combine. Spread the cooked spinach mixture over the bottom of the partially baked crust and top with the bacon. Pour the egg mixture over the bacon and sprinkle with the cheddar cheese and parsley. Bake for 30 to 35 minutes, until the eggs are set and the edges are browned. Remove from the oven and let cool for 5 minutes before cutting into wedges.

Makes **8** Servings

Breakfast wouldn't be the same in our home without my buttermilk pancakes. My little brother is a pancake connoisseur, and he says they are the best pancakes he's ever eaten. This buttermilk syrup all began when my brother-in-law introduced me to his version. I was a fan for life. My boys refer to it as the "candy syrup." The kids get a kick out of helping make the syrup because when it's time to add the baking soda and vanilla, the whole saucepan foams up like a fun science experiment.

One-Bowl Buttermilk Pancakes with Buttermilk Syrup

8	tablespoons (1 stick) unsalted butter, softened
½	cup plus 3 tablespoons granulated sugar
1½	cups buttermilk, divided
1½	teaspoons baking soda, divided
½	teaspoon vanilla extract
1	cup all-purpose flour
1	large egg
1	tablespoon canola oil
¼	teaspoon kosher salt

1. To make the syrup, place the butter, ½ cup of the sugar, and ½ cup of the buttermilk into a medium saucepan over medium heat and stir until melted. Once the syrup starts to boil, add ½ teaspoon of the baking soda and the vanilla, stirring to combine. When the syrup starts to foam, stir, remove from the heat, transfer to a serving dish, and let sit while preparing the pancakes.

2. Lightly spray a large nonstick skillet with cooking spray and heat over medium-low heat.

3. To make the pancakes, add the flour, egg, oil, salt, the remaining 3 tablespoons sugar, 1 cup buttermilk, and 1 teaspoon baking soda to a large bowl and stir until well combined. In batches, pour ¼ cup pancake batter into the hot skillet, spreading with a spoon to even out. Cook until browned, 1 to 2 minutes per side. Transfer the warm pancakes to a plate and cover to keep warm. Drizzle the warm syrup over pancakes and serve.

Makes
4–6
Servings

With my simple blender hollandaise sauce recipe, you don't have to be afraid of trying your own eggs Benedict. This is a great breakfast for special occasions or just a weekend treat. I have my boys hop up to the counter and help pour in the ingredients for the sauce that they will soon be dipping their English muffins into. Crispy bacon, silky-smooth avocado, and rich hollandaise sauce make for a meal the family won't forget.

California-Style Eggs Benedict

8	ounces (2 sticks) unsalted butter
3	large egg yolks
2	teaspoons fresh lemon juice
½	teaspoon kosher salt
¼	teaspoon freshly ground black pepper
¼	teaspoon Worcestershire sauce
1	large avocado, halved
3	English muffins, split
3	tablespoons unsalted butter, softened
6	large eggs
12	strips bacon, cooked until crisp

1. Set up a double boiler by filling a medium saucepan one-quarter full of water, and bring to a boil. Reduce the heat to low and place a heatproof bowl over the saucepan. Do not allow the bowl to touch the water. Spray a large skillet with nonstick cooking spray.

2. To make the hollandaise sauce, in a large microwave-safe dish melt the 2 sticks butter in the microwave until bubbly, 1 to 1½ minutes. Add the egg yolks, lemon juice, salt, pepper, and Worcestershire sauce to a blender and blend until well combined. Slowly drizzle in the melted butter and continue to blend until well combined. Pour the mixture into the double boiler bowl, whisking every 1 minute.

3. Cut the avocado half into 6 slices. Toast the English muffins and spread with the 3 tablespoons butter. Place the prepared skillet over medium heat. In batches, fry the eggs until cooked, about 2 minutes each side. Transfer the eggs on top of the buttered English muffins. Top the eggs with 2 strips of bacon, 2 slices of avocado, and a spoonful of warm hollandaise sauce. Serve immediately.

Makes **6** Servings

I shared this recipe on Picky Palate during Thanksgiving and decided that it was too good to make only once a year. My boys ask for this recipe on a regular basis, and I've found that it's perfect for any breakfast, brunch, or even dinner. It's full of smoky bacon pieces and garlic. We enjoy these potatoes with eggs and pancakes.

Bacon and Onion Pan-Fried Potatoes

1	pound fingerling potatoes
½	pound bacon cut into ½-inch pieces
1	tablespoon unsalted butter
½	cup finely chopped white onion
1	tablespoon minced garlic
¼	cup chopped fresh parsley
¼	teaspoon kosher salt
¼	teaspoon freshly ground black pepper

1. Bring a large pot of water to a boil. Add the potatoes and boil until fork tender, about 10 minutes. Drain and slice lengthwise.

2. Add the bacon to a Dutch oven or medium pot over medium heat and cook, stirring, until browned and crisp, 10 to 15 minutes. Remove the bacon from the pot and discard all but 2 tablespoons of the bacon drippings. Heat the drippings over medium heat with the butter and stir until the butter is melted. Add the onion and cook, stirring, until tender, about 5 minutes. Add the garlic and cook, stirring, for 1 minute. Add the parsley, salt, pepper, sliced potatoes, and bacon and cook, stirring, until warm, about 5 minutes. Reduce the heat to low and serve.

Makes
4
Servings

Here's fair warning—don't leave yourself alone with these biscuits. I spent months developing this delightfully flaky recipe, and I couldn't be happier with it. They are buttery, full of cheddar cheese, and gently seasoned with garlic. They come out of the oven tender, flaky, and begging to be eaten. I love watching my boys and husband dig into these; it's hard to stop after one buttery bite. Enjoy warm with breakfast, brunch, or dinner.

Buttery Cheddar-Garlic Biscuits

1¼	cups all-purpose flour
2	tablespoons baking powder
1	teaspoon kosher salt
¼	teaspoon cream of tartar
¼	teaspoon garlic salt
8	tablespoons (1 stick) cold unsalted butter, diced
¾	cup shredded cheddar cheese
¾	cup buttermilk

1. Preheat the oven to 450°F and spray a large baking sheet with nonstick cooking spray.

2. Add the flour, baking powder, salt, cream of tartar, and garlic salt to a large bowl and stir to combine. With a fork or pastry cutter, cut the butter into the flour mixture until it resembles coarse meal. Stir in the cheddar cheese, then slowly add the buttermilk, stirring until just combined. Pour the dough onto a lightly floured countertop and, with your hands, press to ½-inch thickness. With a 2- to 3-inch biscuit cutter, cut 6 to 8 biscuits and place them on the prepared baking sheet, touching each other. Bake for 10 to 12 minutes, until cooked through.

Makes
6–8
Servings

It puzzles me why people only bake and cook with pumpkin in the fall. I stock up on cans of pumpkin so I can enjoy its deliciousness all year round. This simple pumpkin bread is great for any day of the week and even perfect for bake sales and gifts for friends. This is a simple recipe to have the kids help add ingredients to the mixer. The buttery cinnamon streusel gives a tempting slight crunch on top. Serve with fruit if desired.

Streusel-Topped Pumpkin Bread

¾ cup vegetable oil

2 large eggs

1 tablespoon vanilla extract

1 cup pumpkin purée

1½ cups all-purpose flour, divided

1 cup granulated sugar

1 teaspoon baking soda

¾ teaspoon kosher salt, divided

1 teaspoon ground cinnamon, divided

½ cup packed light brown sugar

4 tablespoons (½ stick) cold unsalted butter, diced

1. Preheat the oven to 350°F and spray a 9×5-inch bread pan with nonstick cooking spray.

2. Add the oil, eggs, and vanilla to the bowl of a stand mixer and beat until well combined, 1 to 1½ minutes. Add the pumpkin and beat on low to combine. Slowly add 1 cup of the flour, the sugar, baking soda, ½ teaspoon of the salt, and ½ teaspoon of the cinnamon and beat on low until just combined. Pour the batter into the prepared bread pan.

3. Add the brown sugar, the remaining ½ cup flour, ½ teaspoon cinnamon, and ¼ teaspoon salt to a medium bowl and mix to combine. With a fork or pastry cutter, cut the butter into the dry ingredients until well combined and crumbly; this takes about 5 minutes. Sprinkle over the bread. Bake for 55 to 65 minutes, until cooked through. Let cool completely before slicing.

Makes **10** Servings

Chapter 2

Get the Party Started

Appetizers to Win Over Guests

No more having to run to the store to buy your spinach dip for parties and get-togethers. This is my go-to spinach dip recipe that will have all of your guests coming back for more. It's quick and simple to prepare, packed with just the right seasonings you most likely already have in your pantry. You can serve this dip in a bowl or large sourdough bread bowl with the center removed and saved for dipping. The kids will get a kick out of making the bread bowl and using it for dipping, even if spinach is something they might not normally love.

Creamy Spinach Dip

2	tablespoons extra-virgin olive oil
1	10-ounce bag fresh spinach leaves
1	tablespoon minced garlic
1	8-ounce package cream cheese, softened
1	8-ounce container sour cream
¼	teaspoon kosher salt
¼	teaspoon freshly ground black pepper
¼	teaspoon garlic salt
1	large sourdough bread bowl

1. Heat the olive oil in a 12-inch skillet over medium heat. Add the spinach and cook, stirring, until wilted, about 5 minutes. Add the garlic and cook, stirring, for 1 minute. Transfer the mixture to a paper towel–lined plate. Let cool for 5 minutes, then with paper towels, press and remove as much liquid as possible from the cooked spinach.

2. Add the cream cheese, sour cream, salt, pepper, garlic salt, and cooked spinach to a mixing bowl, stirring to combine. Transfer to a hollowed-out large sourdough bread bowl. Serve with sourdough bread pieces and/or crackers.

Makes
8–10
Servings

It would be considered a crime if I dared serve an Italian dinner without my Cheesy Garlic Toast. My boys and husband would very likely throw a fit. There is something magical that happens to a loaf of bread when it's lathered with butter, garlic salt, and loads of cheddar cheese. Serve with any Italian meal, soups, and salads.

Cheesy Garlic Toast

1	pound French bread, ciabatta bread, or sourdough bread, cut in half lengthwise
8	tablespoons (1 stick) unsalted butter, softened
1	teaspoon garlic salt
1½	cups shredded cheddar cheese

1. Preheat the broiler with the rack placed 5 to 6 inches below the heat source, and spray a large baking sheet with nonstick cooking spray.

2. Spread the butter evenly over both sides of the cut bread, season with the garlic salt, and top with the cheddar cheese. Transfer the bread to the prepared baking sheet. Place under the broiler, and bake for 3 to 5 minutes, until cheese is melted and bread is toasted; watch carefully because the bread toasts quickly. Remove from the broiler, cut into slices, and serve warm.

Makes **8** Servings

Teedo is a nickname I've had for my dad for as long as I can remember. Teedo is one of the hardest workers I've ever known and is the best dad ever, who also happens to make the absolute best salsa which we insist on having at every family gathering. One of the great things about this salsa is that it's made with simple ingredients that you are likely to have on hand. My dad's secret ingredient is a couple of mashed avocados mixed right in the salsa. Serve with a bowl of crispy tortilla chips and your favorite Mexican meals.

Teedo's Famous Salsa

1	14.5-ounce can diced petite tomatoes
1	10-ounce can diced tomatoes with green chilies
2	avocados, peeled, seeded, and mashed
1½	cups chopped fresh cilantro
1	clove garlic, minced
½	lime, juiced
¼	teaspoon kosher salt
¼	teaspoon freshly ground black pepper

1. Add the petite tomatoes, diced tomatoes, avocados, cilantro, garlic, lime juice, salt, and pepper to a food processor. Pulse to desired consistency.

Makes
10–12
Servings

These warm, toasty rolls layered with mozzarella, basil, and fresh tomatoes are the perfect start to any Italian meal. Warm fresh mozzarella cheese oozes with each bite, while the balsamic vinegar adds the perfect punch of flavor. I like to have the boys add the basil leaves and tomato slices to get them involved. If you are looking for a light dinner, serve the rolls with a simple salad, and dinner is ready.

Toasted Caprese Rolls

9	slices fresh mozzarella (⅛ inch thick)
18	fresh basil leaves
9	slices fresh tomatoes (⅛ inch thick)
9	soft dinner rolls, split
½	teaspoon kosher salt
½	teaspoon freshly ground black pepper
¼	cup extra-virgin olive oil
2	tablespoons balsamic vinegar
4	tablespoons (½ stick) unsalted butter
¼	teaspoon Italian seasoning

1. Preheat the oven to 350°F and spray a 9×13-inch baking dish with nonstick cooking spray.

2. Layer 1 mozzarella slice, 2 basil leaves, and 1 tomato slice on the bottom half of each split roll. Season the tomatoes with a pinch of the salt and pepper. Add the olive oil and vinegar to a small bowl and whisk to combine. Drizzle evenly over the tomatoes. Close the rolls and arrange in the prepared baking dish.

3. Add the butter and Italian seasoning to a small saucepan over medium-low heat to melt, stirring to combine. With a pastry brush, spread the melted butter over the tops of the rolls. Bake for 15 to 20 minutes, until cheese is melted and tops of rolls are golden and toasted.

Makes
4
Servings

It's safe to say that we enjoy Mexican meals often at home. I developed these little bean and cheese burrito cups one night with leftovers, and you would have thought the boys won the lottery with the excitement they showed as they dug in. Watch how something so simple will bring plenty of smiles to your dinner table. Enjoy with any of your favorite Mexican meals.

Mini Bean and Cheese Burrito Cups

2	13.2-ounce cans refrigerated French bread loaf
1	16-ounce can refried beans
1	cup shredded cheddar cheese, divided
¼	cup prepared mild salsa
½	teaspoon kosher salt
¼	teaspoon freshly ground black pepper

1. Preheat the oven to 350°F and spray two 12-count muffin pans with nonstick cooking spray.

2. Unroll both cans of bread dough and cut each into 10 equal 1-inch slices. Press each slice into a 3-inch round, then place into the bottom of the muffin cups. Use your fingers to press the dough down and up the sides of the muffin cups.

3. Add the beans, ½ cup of the cheddar cheese, the salsa, salt, and pepper to a medium mixing bowl and mix to combine. Place a heaping tablespoonful of the bean mixture into the center of each cup. Top evenly with the remaining ½ cup cheddar cheese and bake for 12 to 15 minutes, until edges begin to brown. Let cool for 5 minutes before removing from pan. Serve warm.

Makes
20
Burrito
Cups

There are not many foods I enjoy more than a fresh bowl of guacamole. This recipe I developed is colorful with minimal ingredients to keep the focus on the avocado. Chop your vegetables in advance so you can mash the avocados and prepare the guacamole right before your guests arrive to preserve the freshness and color. The kids get a kick out of grabbing forks to help mash up the avocados. Don't stop with tortilla chips. Try this recipe on top of burgers, chicken breast, and tacos, and inside burritos too.

Party Guacamole

5	large avocados, peeled, seeded, and diced
½	cup quartered and seeded cherry tomatoes
¼	cup chopped fresh cilantro
3	tablespoons fresh lime juice
2	tablespoons finely chopped white onion
½	teaspoon kosher salt
¼	teaspoon freshly ground black pepper

1. Add the avocado to a large bowl. With a fork, mash until just some chunks are still present. Add the tomatoes, cilantro, lime juice, onion, salt, and pepper and stir to combine. This is best if served within 2 hours.

Makes
6–8
Servings

Mona is a nickname I gave my mom years ago for no particular reason; it just stuck! Even the grandkids call her Mona. I've always had a thing for nicknaming my family and I can't explain it. I have fond memories of weekend afternoons as a young girl when Mona would fry up mini corn dogs for my sister and me, and then we'd anxiously wait for them to cool on a napkin-lined plate. It is so fun watching my boys enjoy this recipe just like my sister and I did so many years ago. Make sure you have ketchup and mustard ready for dipping.

Mona's Mini Corn Dogs

3	cups plus 1 tablespoon canola oil
½	cup milk
½	cup cornmeal
1	large egg
1	tablespoon honey
1	tablespoon granulated sugar
1	teaspoon baking soda
½	teaspoon kosher salt
¼	teaspoon garlic salt
¼	teaspoon smoked paprika
5	hot dogs

1. Heat the 3 cups oil in large cast-iron skillet to 350°F on a thermometer.

2. Add the milk, cornmeal, egg, the 1 tablespoon canola oil, honey, sugar, baking soda, salt, garlic salt, and paprika to a large bowl and stir until well combined.

3. Cut the hot dogs into 1-inch pieces. With a toothpick, poke a hot dog and dip into the cornmeal mixture, coating all sides. Carefully drop into the hot oil, frying on both sides until golden brown, about 1 minute per side. Transfer to a paper towel–lined plate to drain. Serve warm.

Makes
20–25
Servings

If you are in need of some cheering up, cook up a big skillet of this smoky and bubbly-hot mac and cheese. It has a way of brightening everyone's day. This recipe is simple and cooks perfectly in a rustic cast-iron skillet. The smoky paprika and buttery crisp bacon topping make for a winning mac and cheese. If the smoky flavor isn't your thing, leave out the smoked paprika and bacon. Feel free to substitute traditional paprika and Canadian bacon or even ham if needed. Serve with your favorite main dish and a simple salad.

Skillet-Baked Mac and Cheese

½	pound elbow pasta
8	tablespoons (1 stick) butter, divided
3	tablespoons all-purpose flour
¾	teaspoon kosher salt
½	teaspoon smoked paprika
¼	teaspoon freshly ground black pepper
1½	cups milk
2	cups shredded cheddar cheese
1	cup Japanese panko bread crumbs
½	pound sliced bacon, cooked until crisp and crumbled (about 1 cup)
¼	cup shredded Parmesan cheese

1. Preheat the oven to 350°F and spray a 9-inch cast-iron skillet with nonstick cooking spray.

2. Cook the pasta according to the package directions, drain, then rinse under cool water to stop the cooking.

3. Melt 3 tablespoons of the butter in a small saucepan over medium heat. Add the flour, salt, paprika, and pepper and whisk to combine. Slowly add the milk, whisking until smooth and thickened, about 5 minutes. Add the cheddar cheese and stir until smooth.

4. Transfer the cooked macaroni to the prepared cast-iron skillet. Pour in the cheese sauce, stirring to combine.

5. In a microwave-safe bowl, melt the remaining 5 tablespoons butter in the microwave. Add the bread crumbs, bacon, and Parmesan cheese and stir to combine. Sprinkle over the mac and cheese, and bake for 25 to 30 minutes, until hot and bubbly.

Makes
6
Servings

If your family enjoys pizza as much as ours does, then this is the appetizer for you. This quick bread is chock-full of pepperoni and two cheeses and only takes about 10 minutes to prepare. I adore simple recipes that come out of the oven looking like a million bucks. You'll find the red marinara sneaking out of every nook and cranny of the loaf, making for gorgeous slices. Enjoy with soup and salad night.

Cheesy Pepperoni Pizza Quick Bread

1	cup all-purpose flour
1½	teaspoons baking powder
½	teaspoon kosher salt
½	teaspoon freshly ground black pepper
¼	teaspoon baking soda
2	large eggs
2	tablespoons extra-virgin olive oil
¾	cup buttermilk
1¾	cups shredded mozzarella cheese, divided
¼	cup shredded Parmesan cheese
1	cup quartered pepperoni slices, about 32 slices
½	cup marinara sauce
1	teaspoon Italian seasoning

1. Preheat the oven to 350°F and spray a 9×5×2¾-inch bread pan with nonstick cooking spray.

2. Add the flour, baking powder, salt, pepper, and baking soda to the bowl of a stand mixer and mix to combine. Slowly add the eggs and olive oil, mixing until just combined. Add the buttermilk, 1½ cups of the mozzarella cheese, the Parmesan cheese, and the pepperoni and mix until just combined. Pour half of the batter into the prepared bread pan. Top evenly with the marinara sauce, then pour the remaining batter over the sauce. Top with the Italian seasoning and the remaining ¼ cup mozzarella cheese.

3. Bake for 45 to 55 minutes, until a toothpick comes out clean from the center. Let cool for 30 minutes before removing from pan. Slice the bread and serve warm or at room temperature.

Makes **8** Servings

Chapter 3

Greens and Things

Sides and Salads

I don't think there is anything that makes my oldest son happier than mashed potatoes. The kid could eat them by the bowlful. I love this quick and simple potato recipe that is doable even during busy weeknights. These mashed potatoes are seasoned just right and are the perfect side for just about any entrée.

Creamy Weeknight Mashed Potatoes

2½	pounds russet potatoes, peeled and diced into about 1-inch pieces
4	tablespoons (½ stick) unsalted butter, softened
4	ounces cream cheese, softened
½	cup warm milk
¼	cup sour cream
1	tablespoon kosher salt
½	teaspoon freshly ground black pepper
½	teaspoon garlic salt

1. Heat the potatoes in a Dutch oven or large pot filled three-quarters full with water over high heat. When the water comes to a boil, cook until the potatoes are fork tender, about 10 minutes. Drain the water, then transfer the potatoes to the bowl of a stand mixer. Beat until the potatoes begin to break up. Add the butter, cream cheese, milk, sour cream, salt, pepper, and garlic salt and beat until creamy.

Makes
6
Servings

When you are not sure what vegetable to serve with dinner, this is your ticket! Not only does this corn have the family swooning over its sweet honey-butter flavors, it takes only a few minutes to prepare. Try adding diced red peppers and chopped cilantro leaves to the melted butter for a Mexican-style corn.

Creamy Honey-Buttered Corn

2	tablespoons unsalted butter
2	tablespoons honey
2½	cups fresh or frozen corn kernels
2	ounces cream cheese
¼	teaspoon kosher salt
¼	teaspoon freshly ground black pepper

1. Place a Dutch oven or medium pot over medium heat. Add the butter and honey and stir until melted. Add the corn and cook, stirring, until hot, about 5 minutes. Add the cream cheese, salt, and pepper and cook, stirring, until melted and combined, 3 to 5 minutes. Serve hot.

Makes **4** Servings

Couscous is such a great side dish it literally takes just minutes to cook and is a great substitute for rice. I cook onions and garlic with fresh spinach and then toss in cooked couscous and fresh Parmesan cheese. Have the kids grab a chair and watch how fast the fresh spinach wilts as you add it to the hot skillet. It's the perfect side with almost any entrée.

Spinach-Parmesan Couscous

1	10-ounce box plain couscous
¼	cup extra-virgin olive oil, divided
5	cups chopped fresh spinach leaves
¼	cup finely chopped white onion
1	tablespoon minced garlic
½	cup shredded Parmesan cheese
½	teaspoon kosher salt
¼	teaspoon freshly ground black pepper

1. Prepare the couscous according to the package directions. Transfer to a large bowl, tossing to fluff.

2. Heat 2 tablespoons of the oil in a Dutch oven or large pot over medium heat. Add the spinach and onion and cook, stirring, until the spinach is wilted, about 5 minutes. Add the garlic and cook, stirring, for 1 minute. Add the cooked couscous, Parmesan cheese, salt, pepper, and the remaining 2 tablespoons of oil and stir to combine. Serve warm.

Makes **6** Servings

Parmesan and bacon are two of my favorite ingredients to cook with. This thinly sliced potato dish is bubbly, rich, creamy, and layered with 3 different cheeses. Au gratin is simply a recipe that is topped with an ingredient that forms a golden crust, usually cheese or bread crumbs. Watch the smiles you get from the family when you place this dish on the kitchen table. These potatoes serve beautifully with chicken, beef, or fish.

3-Cheese and Bacon au Gratin Potatoes

1	tablespoon unsalted butter, softened
1½	pounds russet potatoes, peeled and sliced ⅛ inch thick
1	teaspoon dried thyme
½	teaspoon kosher salt
½	teaspoon freshly ground black pepper
½	teaspoon garlic salt
1	cup shredded mozzarella cheese
½	cup shredded Parmesan cheese
1½	cups heavy cream
¼	pound sliced bacon, cooked until crisp and crumbled (about ½ cup)
½	cup shredded cheddar cheese

1. Preheat the oven to 375°F and grease a 9×13-inch baking dish with the butter.

2. Spread half of the potatoes in the bottom of the prepared baking dish. Season with ½ teaspoon of the thyme, ¼ teaspoon of the salt, ¼ teaspoon of the pepper, and ¼ teaspoon of the garlic salt. Layer with ½ cup of the mozzarella cheese and the Parmesan cheese. Slowly pour ¾ cup of the cream over the first layer. Layer the remaining potatoes on top, season with the remaining ½ teaspoon thyme, ¼ teaspoon salt, ¼ teaspoon pepper, and ¼ teaspoon garlic salt, and sprinkle with the remaining ½ cup mozzarella cheese. Slowly pour the remaining ¾ cup cream over everything, then top with the bacon and cheddar cheese. Bake uncovered, for 45 minutes, until bubbly and the potatoes are fork tender.

Makes **10** Servings

Smashed potatoes are such a fun and messy-looking side dish—the kids really enjoy them. You smash them with your thumb or the tines of a fork and season with salt, pepper, and Parmesan cheese. Experiment with different seasonings and cheeses—any of your favorites will work beautifully. You'll have this recipe on your dinner table in no time, since they only bake 15 minutes in the oven. Serve with your favorite entrée and try dipping in my Homemade Ranch Dressing (page 202) if desired.

Parmesan Roasted Smashed Potatoes

1½	pounds baby potatoes
1	tablespoon extra-virgin olive oil
½	teaspoon kosher salt
¼	teaspoon freshly ground black pepper
3	tablespoons shredded Parmesan cheese

1. Preheat the oven to 375°F and spray a large baking sheet with nonstick cooking spray.

2. Bring a large pot of water to a boil, add the potatoes, and boil until fork tender, about 15 minutes. Drain, transfer to a cutting board, and let the potatoes cool for 10 minutes.

3. Move the warm potatoes to the prepared baking sheet. Using your thumbs or a fork, press each potato to "smash" while trying to keep them intact as much as possible. I find that using my thumbs to smash is easier for keeping potatoes intact. With a pastry brush, lightly brush the tops of the potatoes with the olive oil, season with the salt and pepper, then top with the Parmesan cheese. Bake for 15 minutes, until the cheese is melted and slightly golden. Remove from the oven and serve warm.

Makes
12–15
Servings

I love preparing these "fries" for the kids. Roasting carrots brings out their natural sweetness, and when they're topped with Parmesan cheese you get that delicious sweet-and-salty flavor combination going on. Serve instead of traditional french fries along with my Homemade Ranch Dressing (page 202) for dipping.

Parmesan Roasted Carrot Fries

1	1-pound bag baby carrots
¼	cup shredded Parmesan cheese
2	tablespoons extra-virgin olive oil
½	teaspoon kosher salt
¼	teaspoon freshly ground black pepper
¼	teaspoon garlic salt

1. Preheat the oven to 400°F and line a large baking sheet with parchment paper or a silicone liner.

2. Add the carrots, Parmesan cheese, olive oil, salt, pepper, and garlic salt to a large bowl and stir to combine. Transfer the mixture to the prepared baking sheet and bake for 20 to 25 minutes, until the carrots are fork tender.

Makes
4
Servings

This simple, yet flavor-packed Spanish rice is the perfect side for any Mexican-style dinner. We enjoy this dish with tacos, enchiladas, and burritos. Have the kids help stir in ingredients and watch white rice turn into Spanish rice. Try adding cooked chicken breast, beef, or shrimp along with corn and black beans and turn this side into an entrée.

Spanish Rice

2	cups long-grain white rice
3	tablespoons vegetable or canola oil
1¼	cups finely chopped white onion
2	tablespoons minced garlic
8	ounces tomato sauce
1½	teaspoons kosher salt
1	teaspoon ground cumin
½	teaspoon freshly ground black pepper

1. Bring a large saucepan with 4 cups of water to a boil. Stir in the rice, cover, and reduce heat to low. Simmer until the water is absorbed, about 20 minutes.

2. Heat the vegetable oil in a Dutch oven or large pot over medium heat. Add the onion and cook, stirring, until tender, about 5 minutes. Add the garlic and cook, stirring, for 1 minute. Add the cooked rice, tomato sauce, salt, cumin, and pepper and stir to combine. Reduce the heat to low and serve.

Makes 6–8 Servings

This cornbread baked in a cast-iron skillet is tender, sweet, smoky, and full of cheddar cheese. Have fun with different mix-in ingredients—try adding bacon, onions, peppers, chicken, or beef. If you'd rather not use a cast-iron skillet, you can bake this recipe in an 8- or 9-inch baking dish. This is a great recipe to have the kids help measure and add the ingredients to the mixer. We enjoy this cornbread with chili, BBQ chicken, soups, and salads.

Smoky Cheddar Skillet Cornbread

6	ounces (1½ sticks) unsalted butter, 1 stick softened, ½ stick cold
½	cup granulated sugar
2	large eggs plus 1 egg yolk
1	15-ounce can cream-style corn
1½	cups all-purpose flour, divided
1	cup shredded cheddar cheese
½	cup cornmeal
1¼	teaspoons kosher salt, divided
¼	teaspoon freshly ground black pepper
¼	teaspoon smoked paprika
½	cup packed light brown sugar

1. Preheat the oven to 350°F and spray a 9-inch cast-iron skillet with nonstick cooking spray.

2. Add the softened 1 stick of butter and the sugar to the bowl of a stand mixer and beat on medium speed until light and fluffy. Slowly add the eggs and egg yolk, beating until well combined. Add the corn, 1 cup of the flour, the cheddar cheese, cornmeal, 1 teaspoon of the salt, the pepper, and paprika and beat on low until just combined. Transfer to the prepared skillet.

3. Add the brown sugar and the remaining ½ cup flour and ¼ teaspoon salt to a medium bowl and mix to combine. Cube the ½ stick cold butter and add to the flour mixture. With a pastry cutter or fork, cut the butter into the dry ingredients until well combined and crumbly; this takes about 5 minutes. Sprinkle the streusel on top of the cornbread batter, then bake for 30 to 35 minutes, until cooked through.

Makes **8** Servings

It's not a party unless my beautiful "Granna" has a piping hotpot of her famous baked beans ready for eating. I will never forget the two years my husband I lived with my grandparents while I was in dental hygiene school. My Granna had three-course meals prepared every single night when we came home from a hard day of school and work. I am telling you, it was a dream. We get a good laugh looking back at pictures of those two years. My husband and I had the chubbiest cheeks thanks to Granna's good cooking. Thank you, sweet grandparents, for taking care of us!

Granna's Famous Baked Beans

2	tablespoons extra-virgin olive oil
½	cup finely chopped white onion
1	28-ounce can baked beans
½	cup packed light brown sugar
2	tablespoons molasses
3	strips bacon, cut into 1-inch pieces

1. Preheat the oven to 375°F.

2. Heat the olive oil in a Dutch oven or medium ovenproof pot over medium heat. Add the onion and cook, stirring, until tender, about 5 minutes. Add the baked beans, brown sugar, and molasses, stirring to combine. Top with the bacon pieces and bake for 40 to 45 minutes, until bacon is crisp and beans are bubbly.

Makes
6
Servings

This Picky Palate favorite recipe makes for a great weeknight dinner. Ground turkey is the star here that I've combined with a store-bought teriyaki sauce, some vegetables, and a bag of broccoli slaw that you can find in the produce section of your grocery store by the bagged salad leaves. You can substitute a bag of shredded cabbage if needed. I've made this recipe with 3 cups shredded cooked chicken breast in place of the turkey, which tastes equally delicious. Dinnertime is always more fun for the kids and adults when you get to eat with your hands.

Asian Turkey Lettuce Wraps

2	tablespoons extra-virgin olive oil
1	cup finely chopped onion
1	tablespoon minced garlic
1	pound ground turkey
¼	teaspoon kosher salt
¼	teaspoon freshly ground black pepper
¼	teaspoon garlic salt
1	12-ounce bag broccoli slaw
½	cup teriyaki sauce
1	4-ounce can water chestnuts, drained
1	teaspoon sesame oil
10	to 15 butter or iceberg lettuce leaves

1. Heat the olive oil in a Dutch oven or medium pot over medium heat. Add the onion and cook, stirring, until tender, about 5 minutes. Add the garlic and cook, stirring, for 1 minute. Add the ground turkey, salt, pepper, and garlic salt and cook, stirring and breaking up meat, until browned.

2. Add the broccoli slaw, teriyaki sauce, water chestnuts, and sesame oil and cook, stirring, until heated through, 8 to 10 minutes. Reduce the heat to low and serve wrapped in cold, crisp lettuce leaves.

Makes
10–15
Servings

It's nice to have ingredients on hand to whip up a simple salad with dinner every night. I've shared my favorite salad toppings along with a fresh crisp lemon dressing that takes 30 seconds to prepare. Have the kids help pick out their favorite vegetables from the grocery store and help assemble the salad. Use my recipe as just a guide, and add your favorite salad toppings that make your family happy. Try with my Homemade Ranch Dressing (page 202) as an alternate to the lemon dressing, if desired.

Simple Green Salad

1	5-ounce bag mixed greens
10	ounces grape tomatoes
1	cup peeled, quartered, and sliced cucumber
1	cup peeled and shredded carrot
½	cup chopped mini sweet peppers
½	cup crumbled feta cheese
	Simple Lemon Dressing (see page 202)

1. Add the mixed greens to a large salad bowl. Top evenly with the tomatoes, cucumber, carrot, sweet peppers, and feta cheese. Drizzle the dressing over the salad and toss, or serve the dressing on the side.

Makes
6
Servings

If you haven't cooked with quinoa yet, pick some up next time you are at the grocery store. It is good for you and takes no time at all to prepare. Don't be afraid of the unusual name—it tastes much like rice, and the kids think it's fun to try to pronounce "quinoa" correctly. For a busy mom, it's always nice to have recipes that don't keep you in the kitchen for long. Serve with any lunch or dinner, and enjoy chilled or at room temperature. This is a great salad to prepare the day before serving, as it tastes better the longer it marinates in its dressing.

Southwest Quinoa Salad

2	cups quinoa
1	15-ounce can black beans, drained and rinsed
1	15-ounce can corn, drained
1	cup halved cherry tomatoes
1	6-ounce can small pitted ripe black olives
½	cup finely chopped mini sweet peppers
½	cup chopped fresh cilantro leaves
1½	teaspoons kosher salt, divided
½	teaspoon freshly ground black pepper
½	cup extra-virgin olive oil
¼	cup fresh lime juice
½	teaspoon granulated sugar
¼	teaspoon ground cumin

1. Rinse the quinoa in warm water and bring 4 cups of water to a boil in a 2-quart saucepan. Add the quinoa, bring back to a boil, cover, and cook over medium heat until the water is absorbed, about 12 minutes. Remove from the heat, fluff with a fork, and let stand for 15 minutes. Transfer to a large mixing bowl. Add the black beans, corn, tomatoes, olives, sweet peppers, cilantro, 1 teaspoon of the salt, and the pepper and stir to combine.

2. To make the dressing, add the olive oil, lime juice, sugar, cumin, and the remaining ½ teaspoon salt to a medium bowl, whisk to combine, then pour over the quinoa and stir to combine. Serve at room temperature or refrigerate until ready to serve.

Makes
8–10
Servings

This colorful, crunchy, and flavor-packed salad is prepared on a regular basis in our home. It's great when you need to bring a salad for a party and even better to have in the refrigerator to snack on during the day for lunch or dinner. Whatever the occasion, this chilled salad is a huge hit.

Veggie, Feta, and Couscous Salad

2	5.9-ounce boxes plain couscous
2	cups broccoli florets
1	cup grape tomatoes
½	cup chopped mini sweet peppers
½	cup crumbled feta cheese
¼	cup shredded Parmesan cheese
¼	cup chopped fresh parsley
½	cup extra-virgin olive oil
½	lemon, juiced
½	teaspoon kosher salt
¼	teaspoon freshly ground black pepper

1. Cook the couscous according to the package directions, then transfer to a large bowl to cool, stirring every couple of minutes, for about 10 minutes.

2. Add the broccoli florets, tomatoes, sweet peppers, feta cheese, Parmesan cheese, and parsley to the couscous and stir to combine.

3. To make the dressing, add the olive oil, lemon juice, salt, and pepper to a small bowl, whisk to combine, then pour over the couscous and vegetables. Stir to combine and serve, or chill until ready to use.

Makes
8–10
Servings

Chicken salad is such a versatile salad—it can be enjoyed on sandwiches, salads, crackers, and even right out of the bowl with a fork. I've developed a creamy chicken salad with my favorite seasonings and added some salty cashews for texture. Any of your favorite nuts would make a great substitute. With this recipe being prepared in one bowl, it's a great opportunity to have the kids help measure, add the ingredients, and mix it all together. Serve as desired.

Cashew Chicken Salad

2½	cups shredded cooked chicken breast
½	cup finely chopped celery
½	cup mayonnaise
½	cup coarsely chopped lightly salted cashews
¼	cup chopped fresh parsley
¼	cup dill pickle relish
2	tablespoons minced white onion
1	tablespoon fresh lemon juice
1	tablespoon minced garlic
½	teaspoon dried thyme
½	teaspoon kosher salt
½	teaspoon freshly ground black pepper

1. Add all ingredients to a large bowl, mixing until well combined. Serve chilled or at room temperature.

Makes
6–8
Servings

If you've never had homemade crispy potato chips, you are in for quite a treat. Not only are they delicious, but they take under 20 minutes to prepare. Get creative with different flavors—take a look at your spice rack and have some fun. Try Parmesan cheese, taco seasoning, dry ranch dressing seasoning, or even truffle oil. Just about anything goes.

Homemade Potato Chips

	Canola oil
2	large russet potatoes
½	teaspoon kosher salt

1. Heat 3 inches of canola oil in a medium Dutch oven or other pot over medium heat to 350°F on a thermometer.

2. Thinly slice the potatoes to about ⅛-inch slices. It is helpful to use a mandoline when possible. Carefully drop the potato slices into the hot oil in batches, about 1 cup at a time. Cook and stir the potatoes until golden brown on each side, 3 to 4 minutes per batch. Remove with a slotted spoon or a metal spider strainer to a paper towel–lined bowl or plate and season with the salt. Best if eaten within 2 hours.

Makes
4
Servings

Chapter 4

Home Is Where the Chicken Dinner Is

Everyone needs to indulge in good, down-home fried chicken from time to time. I have developed a perfectly crisp chicken that will have you savoring every bite. Don't be afraid of the hot sauce—it adds a punch of flavor without a noticeable heat. The kids love hopping up to the counter with me to help dip the chicken into each bowl. Enjoy this dish with Creamy Weeknight Mashed Potatoes (page 45) or Skillet-Baked Mac and Cheese (page 38).

Crispy Buttermilk Fried Chicken

64	ounces vegetable oil
1	pound chicken drumsticks
1¼	teaspoons kosher salt, divided
¾	teaspoon freshly ground black pepper, divided
1	cup buttermilk
1	tablespoon hot sauce
1	cup all-purpose flour
½	teaspoon smoked paprika

1. Heat the oil in a Dutch oven or large pot over medium heat until the temperature reaches 350°F.

2. Season the drumsticks with ½ teaspoon of the salt and ¼ teaspoon of the pepper. Add the buttermilk and hot sauce to a large bowl and stir to combine. Add the drumsticks, covering them in buttermilk.

3. Add the flour, paprika, ½ teaspoon of the remaining salt, and the remaining ½ teaspoon pepper to a large bowl and mix to combine.

4. Remove the chicken from the buttermilk, letting the excess drip back into the bowl, then dredge in the flour, turning to coat. Dip back into the buttermilk and back into the flour, turning and coating all sides. Carefully drop the chicken into the hot oil and cook until golden brown and cooked through, 15 to 18 minutes. Transfer the chicken to a brown paper bag or paper towel–lined plate to drain. Season with the remaining ¼ teaspoon salt and cool for 5 minutes before serving.

Makes
4
Servings

My boys are all smiles when I tell them we are having a spaghetti night, which is probably why I make this dish so often. Adding a touch of cream and shredded chicken to the sauce gives traditional spaghetti a whole new look and flavor. If you are short on time, use your favorite jarred pasta sauce in place of my homemade sauce. Serve with Cheesy Garlic Toast (page 31) and a simple salad.

Creamy Chicken-Spaghetti Bake

1	pound thin spaghetti
2	tablespoons extra-virgin olive oil
1	cup finely chopped white onion
1	tablespoon minced garlic
2	cups shredded cooked chicken breast
1	28-ounce can crushed tomatoes
¼	cup chopped fresh basil leaves
¾	teaspoon kosher salt
½	teaspoon freshly ground black pepper
¼	teaspoon dried Italian seasoning
¼	cup grated Parmesan cheese
1½	cups shredded mozzarella cheese

1. Preheat the oven to 350°F and spray a 9×13-inch baking dish with nonstick cooking spray.

2. Cook the spaghetti according to the package directions, drain, and set aside.

3. Heat the oil in a Dutch oven or large pot over medium heat. Add onion and cook, stirring, until tender, about 5 minutes. Add the garlic and cook, stirring, for 1 minute. Add the chicken, tomatoes, basil, salt, pepper, and Italian seasoning and stir to combine. Reduce the heat to low and simmer for 10 minutes.

4. Cut the cooked spaghetti in half with kitchen scissors, just a few cuts. This makes it easier to serve after it is baked. Add to the sauce.

5. Transfer chicken and spaghetti mixture to the prepared baking dish. Top with the Parmesan and mozzarella cheeses. Bake for 20 to 25 minutes, until the cheese is melted. Let cool for 5 minutes before serving.

Makes **6** Servings

These quick-to-prepare chicken enchiladas are great for busy weeknights. Rotisserie chicken from your grocery store can be used here, a great way to save yourself a little time from baking your own chicken. The kids can help layer the enchilada toppings over each tortilla. My boys love peeking into the oven to watch the cheese melt. Serve with Mini Bean and Cheese Burrito Cups (page 35), a bowl of tortilla chips, and Teedo's Famous Salsa (page 33).

Chicken, Zucchini, and Black Bean Enchiladas

2	tablespoons extra-virgin olive oil
1	cup sliced zucchini
½	cup finely chopped white onion
2	cups shredded cooked chicken breast
1	15-ounce can black beans, drained and rinsed
½	cup mild prepared salsa of your choice
1¼	teaspoons ground cumin
1	10-ounce can mild red enchilada sauce
½	cup sour cream
12	corn tortillas
½	cup shredded cheddar cheese

1. Preheat the oven to 350°F and spray a 9×13-inch baking dish with nonstick cooking spray.

2. Heat the oil in a Dutch oven or medium pot over medium heat. Add the zucchini and onion and cook, stirring, until tender, about 5 minutes. Add the chicken, beans, salsa, and cumin and stir to combine. Reduce the heat to low.

3. Add the enchilada sauce and sour cream to a small saucepan over medium-low heat and stir until well combined.

4. Heat a few tortillas at a time in a microwave oven until warm, about 60 seconds. Place ¼ cup of the chicken filling in the center of each tortilla. Gently roll and place seam side down in the prepared baking dish. Continue filling and rolling until all 12 tortillas are used. Sprinkle the remaining chicken and vegetables over the rolled tortillas, then pour the warm enchilada sauce over the top. Sprinkle with the cheddar cheese, then bake for 25 to 30 minutes, until the cheese is melted and beginning to brown. Remove and let cool for 5 minutes before serving.

Makes **6** Servings

Chicken pot pie is one of those ultimate comfort foods that just make you feel good. We love making these pot pies as individual servings by using 2-cup ramekins so everyone has his or her own little pie. Be sure to remind the kids to be careful when the ramekins are warm. Use the vegetable suggestions you see in my recipe as just a recommendation. Use any vegetables you have in the fridge or freezer that need to be used up. You can use my Homemade Pie Crust (page 203) in place of the puff pastry if desired. Serve with a simple salad.

Cheesy Chicken Pot Pies

2	cups baby red potatoes
3	tablespoons extra-virgin olive oil
1½	cups finely chopped white onion
1	cup finely chopped carrot
1	cup celery
1	tablespoon minced garlic
2	cups shredded cooked chicken breast
1	cup frozen peas
8	tablespoons (1 stick) butter
½	cup all-purpose flour
½	teaspoon salt
¼	teaspoon freshly ground black pepper
3½	cups reduced-sodium chicken broth
1½	cups shredded cheddar cheese
2	sheets frozen puff pastry, at room temperature

1. Preheat the oven to 350°F and spray six 2-cup ramekins with nonstick cooking spray.

2. Add the baby potatoes to a large pot of water, bring to a boil, and cook until fork tender, about 10 minutes. Drain and set aside.

3. Heat the oil in a large Dutch oven or large pot over medium heat. Add the onion, carrot, and celery and cook, stirring, until tender, 8 to 10 minutes. Add the garlic and cook, stirring, for 1 minute. Add the chicken and peas and cook, stirring, for 5 minutes, then reduce the heat to low.

4. Melt the butter in a medium saucepan over medium-high heat. Add the flour, salt, and pepper and whisk for 1 minute. Slowly add the chicken broth, whisking until thick and creamy, about 3 minutes. Add the cheddar cheese, stirring until melted. Pour the sauce over the chicken and vegetables.

5. Divide the filling among the prepared ramekins. Cut the puff pastry into six 5-inch rounds and place over the filling. Bake for 25 to 30 minutes, until puff pastry is golden brown. Let the pies sit for 10 minutes and serve warm.

Makes
6
Servings

This simple and flavor-packed grilled chicken pasta is one of our favorite weeknight dinners. It's amazing how much flavor roasted red peppers bring to this incredibly easy sauce. Let the kids hunt for their favorite shaped pasta at the grocery store to get them involved with dinner. Enjoy with a simple green salad and a steamed vegetable of your choice.

Creamy Roasted Red Pepper and Basil Bowtie Pasta with Grilled Chicken

2	large boneless skinless chicken cutlets
½	cup prepared Italian dressing of your choice
1	15-ounce jar roasted red peppers, drained
1	tablespoon minced garlic
½	cup heavy cream
8	fresh basil leaves, chopped
1	pound bowtie pasta
4	tablespoons (½ stick) butter
¼	cup freshly grated Parmesan cheese

1. Place the chicken and dressing in a large zip-top bag and marinate for 20 to 30 minutes.

2. Preheat an outdoor or indoor grill to medium-high heat.

3. Add the roasted red peppers and garlic to a food processor and pulse until smooth. Heat in a small saucepan over medium-low heat. Add the heavy cream and basil leaves and stir to combine.

4. Cook the pasta according to the package directions. Drain, then add the pasta back to the pot over low heat. Add the butter and Parmesan cheese, stirring to melt the butter.

5. Remove the marinated chicken from the bag and grill until cooked through, about 5 minutes on each side. Let the chicken rest for 5 minutes, then slice into ½-inch strips. Place the pasta in a large serving bowl. Top with the sauce and grilled chicken strips.

Makes **6** Servings

I love how strips of bacon look wrapped around each little chicken tender in this recipe. The kids can help by wrapping each strip of bacon around the chicken strips. Since chicken tenders are so small, they take no time at all to cook. I like to serve this dish with my Creamy Weeknight Mashed Potatoes (page 45) and a side of my Parmesan Roasted Carrot Fries (page 50).

Bacon-Wrapped Honey-Mustard Chicken Tenders

8	to 10 chicken tenders
½	teaspoon kosher salt
¼	teaspoon freshly ground black pepper
¼	cup yellow mustard
2	tablespoons honey
16	to 20 precooked bacon strips

1. Preheat the oven to 350°F and spray a baking rack placed over a cookie sheet with nonstick cooking spray.

2. Season both sides of the chicken tenders evenly with the salt and pepper. Add the mustard and honey to a small bowl and mix to combine. With a pastry brush, spread the mustard sauce over both sides of the chicken. Wrap 2 pieces of bacon around each chicken tender and place onto prepared baking rack. Bake for 25 to 30 minutes, until the chicken is cooked through.

Makes **6–8** Servings

I love putting new spins on traditional family favorite meals. My kids could have tacos every single week and be completely satisfied. I used a variety of our favorite taco ingredients to develop this simple and tasty taco bake. Serve with bowls of chips, Teedo's Famous Salsa (page 33), and a simple salad.

Salsa Verde Chicken Taco Bake

2	tablespoons extra-virgin olive oil
1	cup diced red bell pepper
1	cup quartered and sliced zucchini
½	cup chopped white onion
4	cups shredded rotisserie chicken
1	tablespoon minced garlic
1	24-ounce container sour cream
1	16-ounce jar mild salsa verde
½	teaspoon ground cumin
¼	teaspoon kosher salt
¼	teaspoon freshly ground black pepper
24	corn tortillas
1	cup shredded cheddar cheese

1. Preheat the oven to 350°F and spray a 9×13-inch baking dish with nonstick cooking spray.

2. Heat the olive oil in a Dutch oven or large pot over medium heat. Add the bell pepper, zucchini, and onion and cook, stirring, until tender, about 5 minutes. Add the chicken and garlic and cook, stirring, until hot, about 5 minutes. Add the sour cream, salsa, cumin, salt, and pepper, stir to combine, then reduce the heat to low.

3. Cut the tortillas into eighths. Layer half of the cut tortillas in the bottom of the prepared baking dish. Pour half of the chicken mixture over the tortillas. Place the remaining tortillas over the chicken, then pour the remaining chicken mixture over. Sprinkle with the cheddar cheese and bake for 30 to 40 minutes, until cheese is melted and slightly browned. Serve immediately.

Makes
8
Servings

Zesty chicken taco filling enclosed in a flaky puff pastry makes for a family-pleasing Mexican dinner. Puff pastry is one of those products I make sure I always have on hand in the freezer. It's great for simple dinners during busy weeknights. Serve these taco pockets with a bowl of chips, Teedo's Famous Salsa (page 33), and a simple salad.

Flaky Chicken Taco Pockets

2	tablespoons extra-virgin olive oil
½	cup finely chopped white onion
1	tablespoon minced garlic
2	cups shredded cooked chicken breast
1	10-ounce can diced tomatoes with green chilies
¼	cup chopped fresh cilantro leaves
1	tablespoon fresh lime juice
½	teaspoon kosher salt
½	teaspoon ground cumin
¼	teaspoon freshly ground black pepper
2	sheets frozen puff pastry, at room temperature
¼	cup shredded cheddar cheese

1. Preheat the oven to 350°F and spray a large baking sheet with nonstick cooking spray.

2. Add the olive oil to a large skillet over medium heat. Add the onion and cook, stirring, until tender, about 5 minutes. Add the garlic and cook, stirring, for 1 minute. Add the chicken, tomatoes, cilantro, lime juice, salt, cumin, and pepper and stir to combine. Cook, stirring, until hot, about 5 minutes, and then reduce the heat to low.

3. Unfold each sheet of puff pastry onto a clean countertop. Cut both sheets into 4 equal squares and place onto the prepared baking sheet. Place ¼ cup of the chicken mixture in the center of each square, top with 1 tablespoon of cheese, and fold the corners of pastry over the filling, forming a triangle shape. With the tines of a fork, firmly press and seal the pastry edges to enclose the filling. Poke a couple of holes in the top of the pastry to allow steam to escape. Bake for 25 to 30 minutes, until the pastry is golden brown and cooked through. Remove and let cool for 5 minutes before serving.

Makes **8** Servings

I like to call this recipe "dinner in a flash." It is packed with great pesto flavor and requires minimal work in the kitchen. Shredded rotisserie chicken works great in this dish, as does a large can of chunk chicken you can find at your grocery store by the cans of tuna fish to save time from baking your own chicken. Have the kids toss in some green peas or steamed broccoli for extra vegetables, color, and texture. Enjoy with a simple salad and Cheesy Garlic Toast (page 31).

Creamy Chicken Pesto Penne Dinner

1	pound penne
1	8-ounce package cream cheese, softened
1	cup milk, divided
2	cups shredded cooked chicken breast
¾	cup prepared pesto
¼	teaspoon kosher salt
¼	teaspoon freshly ground black pepper
½	cup pine nuts (optional)

1. Cook the penne according to the package directions. Drain and run under cool water to stop the cooking.

2. Add the cream cheese and ¾ cup of the milk to a Dutch oven or large pot over medium-low heat, stirring until smooth and melted. Add the chicken, pesto, salt, pepper, and cooked pasta and stir to combine, then reduce the heat to low. Add the remaining ¼ cup milk to loosen the sauce right before serving. Garnish each plate of pasta with pine nuts, if desired.

Makes
6
Servings

No need to go out for chicken tenders after trying my recipe. It's dipped in buttermilk and pan fried for an irresistible crunchy Parmesan crust that keeps little fingers coming back for more. Serve with my Parmesan Roasted Carrot Fries (page 49) and Creamy Weeknight Mashed Potatoes (page 45). Dip with my Homemade Ranch Dressing (page 202), if desired.

Crispy Buttermilk Parmesan Chicken Tenders

6 to 8 chicken tenders (about 1½ pounds)

1 teaspoon kosher salt, divided

½ teaspoon freshly ground black pepper, divided

1½ cups buttermilk

1 large egg

1 cup all-purpose flour

1½ cups Japanese panko bread crumbs

½ cup grated Parmesan cheese

½ teaspoon dried thyme leaves, crushed

6 tablespoons extra-virgin olive oil, divided

1. Season both sides of the chicken tenders with ½ teaspoon of the salt and ¼ teaspoon of the pepper. Add the buttermilk and egg to a shallow dish and whisk to combine. Add the flour and the remaining ½ teaspoon salt and ¼ teaspoon pepper to a second shallow dish and stir to combine. Add the bread crumbs, Parmesan cheese, and thyme to a third shallow dish and stir to combine.

2. Dip the chicken first in the buttermilk, second into the flour, third into the buttermilk again, and fourth, press into the bread crumb mixture. Place all of the breaded chicken tenders onto a large plate.

3. Heat 3 tablespoons of the olive oil in a large skillet over medium heat. Add half of the chicken to the hot oil and cook until golden on each side, 4 to 5 minutes. Add the remaining 3 tablespoons olive oil and cook the second batch the same way. Serve warm.

Makes
6–8
Servings

No need to heat the oven for this simple smoky and creamy pasta dish. Preparation is done right on the stovetop in less than 30 minutes. If time is short, use rotisserie chicken from the grocery store instead of baking your own chicken. Once the vegetables are chopped, have the kids help measure them and add to the pot. Serve this recipe with a simple salad and Cheesy Garlic Toast (page 31).

Chicken, Corn, and Black Bean Pasta in Fire-Roasted Tomato Cream Sauce

1	pound farfalle pasta
2	tablespoons extra-virgin olive oil
½	cup finely diced white onion
1	tablespoon minced garlic
2	cups diced cooked chicken breast
1	15-ounce can black beans, drained and rinsed
1	cup fresh corn kernels
¼	cup chopped fresh cilantro leaves
2	14-ounce cans fire-roasted diced tomatoes
½	cup heavy cream
¼	teaspoon kosher salt
¼	teaspoon freshly ground black pepper
¼	teaspoon garlic salt

1. Cook the farfalle pasta according to the package directions, drain, run under cold water to stop the cooking, and set aside.

2. Heat the olive oil in a Dutch oven or large pot over medium heat. Add the onion and cook, stirring, until tender, about 5 minutes. Add the garlic and cook, stirring, for 1 minute. Add the chicken, beans, corn, and cilantro, stirring until heated through, about 3 minutes. Reduce the heat to low.

3. Add the tomatoes to a food processor and pulse until nearly smooth. Add the tomatoes and cooked pasta to the chicken mixture and stir to combine. Add the heavy cream, salt, pepper, and garlic salt. Cook, stirring, until heated, about 5 minutes, and serve.

Makes
6–8
Servings

Chicken and rice are two foods that go together well and make for a quick meal. This simple yet flavorful dinner has a little something for everyone. The colorful vegetables and shredded chicken are tossed with a ranch and Romano cheese–seasoned rice. Have the kids help measure out the vegetables and add them to the pot. My boys love the vibrant colors of this dish. Use any vegetables that you have on hand in your refrigerator. Enjoy with a simple salad.

Romano-Ranch Chicken and Rice Skillet Dinner

1	cup long-grain white rice
2	large boneless skinless chicken breasts
1	0.4-ounce packet ranch dressing mix, divided
¼	cup extra-virgin olive oil
6	cups fresh spinach leaves, chopped
1¼	cups finely chopped white onion
1	cup peeled and diced carrot
½	cup diced green bell pepper
6	cloves garlic, minced
1	teaspoon kosher salt
¼	teaspoon freshly ground black pepper
¼	teaspoon garlic salt
½	cup shredded Romano cheese

1. Preheat the oven to 350°F and spray an 8×8-inch baking dish with nonstick cooking spray.

2. Bring a large saucepan with 2 cups of water to a boil. Stir in the rice, cover, and reduce heat to low. Simmer for 20 minutes, until the water is absorbed, and set aside.

3. Season both sides of the chicken breasts with 1 teaspoon of the ranch dressing mix and place in the prepared baking dish. Bake for 30 to 35 minutes, until the chicken is cooked through. Remove and let rest for 10 minutes.

4. Heat the olive oil in a large skillet over medium heat. Add the spinach, onion, carrot, bell pepper, and garlic and cook, stirring, until tender, 5 to 7 minutes. Add the rice, season with the salt, pepper, and garlic salt, and stir to combine.

5. Cut both chicken breasts into ½ inch cubes and add to the rice mixture. Season with the remaining ranch dressing mix, add the Romano cheese, and stir to combine. Reduce the heat to low and serve.

Makes **4** Servings

I have memories of blazing hot Arizona summers at my sister's pool eating bowlfuls of these peanut noodles. I have made them dozens and dozens of times and have enjoyed every bit of it. The beauty of this recipe is you can enjoy these noodles chilled or warm, whatever you are in the mood for. To save time from baking your own chicken, pick up a rotisserie chicken from the grocery store, if desired.

Peanut-Ginger Chicken Noodles

1	pound thin spaghetti
½	cup creamy peanut butter
¼	cup reduced-sodium soy sauce
2	tablespoons packed light brown sugar
1½	tablespoons peeled and grated fresh ginger
1	tablespoon minced garlic
1	tablespoon rice wine vinegar
1	cup hot water
2	tablespoons extra-virgin olive oil
½	cup finely chopped white onion
½	cup chopped red bell pepper
2	cups shredded cooked chicken breast
½	cup chopped fresh cilantro leaves
½	teaspoon kosher salt
¼	teaspoon freshly ground black pepper
2	tablespoons toasted sesame seeds (optional)

1. Cook the spaghetti according to the package directions, drain, and run under cold water to stop the cooking.

2. Add the peanut butter, soy sauce, brown sugar, ginger, garlic, and vinegar to a blender and blend until smooth. Slowly add the hot water, blending until smooth.

3. Heat the olive oil in a Dutch oven or large pot over medium heat. Add the onion and bell pepper and cook, stirring, until tender, about 5 minutes. Add the chicken, cilantro, salt, pepper, cooked spaghetti, and peanut sauce and stir to combine. Reduce the heat to low and cook, stirring, for 5 minutes. Serve warm or chilled, topped with toasted sesame seeds, if desired.

Makes **6** Servings

My sister has told me on numerous occasions that this is one of her favorite recipes of mine. I remember developing this recipe in my Arizona kitchen a few years ago, just knowing it was going to be delicious. Shredded BBQ chicken is baked right on top of creamy, smoky mac and cheese. Check your grocery store's refrigerated section for prepared shredded BBQ chicken, if you are short on time. Enjoy with a simple salad.

Smoked Cheddar BBQ Chicken Mac

1	pound small dry pasta of your choice
5	tablespoons butter
5	tablespoons all-purpose flour
½	teaspoon salt
½	teaspoon freshly ground black pepper
4	cups 2% milk
6	cups shredded smoked cheddar cheese, divided
2	cups shredded cooked chicken breast
½	cup prepared BBQ sauce

1. Preheat the oven to 350°F and spray a 9×13-inch baking dish with nonstick cooking spray.

2. Cook the pasta according to the package directions, drain, run under cold water to stop the cooking, and set aside.

3. Melt the butter in a Dutch oven or large pot over medium heat. Add the flour, salt, and pepper and cook, whisking for 1 minute. Slowly add the milk, whisking until smooth. Increase the heat to medium high, stirring continuously until the liquid thickens and comes to a low boil, about 5 minutes. Reduce the heat to low and add 5 cups of the cheese, stirring until smooth and melted. Add the cooked pasta and stir to combine. Pour the mac and cheese into the prepared baking dish.

4. Add the chicken and BBQ sauce to a medium bowl and stir to combine. Spread the chicken evenly over the mac and cheese, then sprinkle with the remaining 1 cup cheddar cheese. Bake for 25 to 30 minutes, until cheese is melted, and serve immediately.

Makes **8** Servings

I have to admit, I am a huge fan of traditional chicken Parmesan. In fact, I order it just about every time we go to an Italian restaurant. The oozing mozzarella, warm breaded chicken breast, and meaty marinara gets me every time. This pasta dish has all of those delicious ingredients, along with rigatoni pasta. Kids as well as adults will enjoy this family-style meal. Serve with a simple salad and Cheesy Garlic Toast (page 31).

Chicken Parmesan Rigatoni Bake

4	large boneless skinless chicken breasts
½	cup all-purpose flour
1	teaspoon salt
½	teaspoon freshly ground black pepper
2	large eggs
½	cup Italian bread crumbs
½	cup Japanese panko bread crumbs
½	cup grated Parmesan cheese
1	pound rigatoni
2	tablespoons extra-virgin olive oil
1	cup finely chopped white onion
½	cup diced red bell pepper
2	cloves garlic, minced
1	26-ounce jar pasta sauce
1½	cups shredded mozzarella cheese

1. Preheat the oven to 350°F and spray a baking rack placed over a 9×13-inch baking dish with nonstick cooking spray.

2. Pound the chicken breasts to an even ½ inch thickness with a meat mallet or rolling pin.

3. Add the flour, salt, and pepper to a shallow dish and mix to combine. Add the eggs and 2 tablespoons of water to a separate shallow dish and whisk to combine. Add the bread crumbs and Parmesan cheese to a third shallow dish. Dip the chicken into the flour, then the eggs, then into the bread crumb mixture, pressing gently. Place the coated chicken on the prepared baking rack. Bake for 23 to 25 minutes, until chicken is cooked through.

4. Cook the rigatoni according to the package directions. Drain and run under cold water to stop the cooking.

5. Heat the olive oil in a Dutch oven or large pot over medium heat. Add the onion and bell pepper and cook, stirring, until tender, about 5 minutes. Add the garlic and cook, stirring, for 1 minute. Add the pasta sauce, reduce the heat to low, add the cooked pasta, stir to combine, and pour into the prepared baking dish.

6. Top with the cheese and bake for 20 to 25 minutes, until hot and bubbly. Cut the chicken into strips, place over pasta, and serve.

Makes
6
Servings

Taquitos are certainly considered a family-friendly food. Kids love eating with their hands, and these are perfect for it. I've seasoned shredded chicken breast with some of my favorite Mexican ingredients and rolled it into flour tortillas that are baked until crunchy and golden brown. This recipe is perfect for busy weeknights and great for weekend finger food too. Enjoy with my Mini Bean and Cheese Burrito Cups (page 35) and Spanish Rice (page 31).

Weeknight Shredded Chicken Taquitos

2	tablespoons extra-virgin olive oil
½	cup finely chopped onion
¼	cup finely chopped red bell pepper
1	tablespoon minced garlic
2	cups shredded cooked chicken breast
1	10-ounce can diced tomatoes with green chilies
3	tablespoons finely chopped cilantro leaves
½	teaspoon kosher salt
½	teaspoon ground cumin
¼	teaspoon freshly ground black pepper
10	10-inch flour tortillas
1½	cups shredded cheddar cheese

1. Preheat the oven to 400°F and spray a large baking sheet with nonstick cooking spray.

2. Heat the olive oil in a Dutch oven or medium pot over medium heat. Add the onion and bell pepper and cook, stirring, until tender, about 5 minutes. Add the garlic and cook, stirring, for 1 minute. Add the chicken, tomatoes, cilantro, salt, cumin, and pepper and cook, stirring, until hot, about 3 minutes. Reduce the heat to low to keep warm.

3. Add ¼ cup of the chicken filling to the center of each tortilla and top with 2 tablespoons of the cheddar cheese. Roll tightly and place seam side down onto the prepared baking sheet. Bake for 25 to 30 minutes, until the tortillas are crispy.

Makes **10** Servings

A little spice is always nice. It's amazing what one tablespoon of adobo sauce from a can of chipotle peppers can do. You can find cans of chipotle peppers in the Mexican aisle of most grocery stores. This is a great weeknight dinner, and you can control how much heat to add in. If you enjoy your food spicy, start with 2 tablespoons of adobo sauce and test from there. My boys like to help add the mozzarella cheese to the pot and watch it melt as I stir. We enjoy this dinner with a simple salad.

Creamy Chipotle Chicken Tortellini with White Beans and Cilantro

1	8-ounce package dry cheese-filled tortellini
4	tablespoons (½ stick) butter
¼	cup all-purpose flour
¼	teaspoon salt
¼	teaspoon freshly ground black pepper
2	cups skim milk
2	cups shredded mozzarella cheese
2	cups shredded cooked chicken breast
1	14-ounce can white beans, drained and rinsed
¼	cup chopped fresh cilantro leaves
1	tablespoon adobo sauce, from can of chipotle peppers

1. Cook the tortellini according to the package directions, drain, and run under cold water to stop the cooking.

2. Melt the butter in a Dutch oven or large pot over medium heat. Add the flour, salt, and pepper and whisk to combine. Increase the heat to medium high and slowly add the milk, whisking until thickened, about 5 minutes.

3. Reduce the heat to low and add the shredded mozzarella cheese, stirring until melted and smooth. Add the chicken, beans, cilantro, adobo sauce, and cooked tortellini, stirring and cooking until heated through, about 5 minutes.

Makes
6
Servings

I have made this casserole so many times I could quite possibly prepare it with my eyes closed. The cheesy sauce that is added to the wild rice and vegetables is good enough to eat with a spoon right out of the saucepan. Have the kids help measure and add the vegetables to the pot. My boys love helping with this recipe. This is a great recipe if you are feeding a group or want to enjoy leftovers for a couple days. Enjoy with a simple salad.

Cheesy Chicken and Wild Rice Casserole

3	tablespoons extra-virgin olive oil
1½	cups peeled and diced carrot
1¼	cups finely chopped white onion
1	cup diced celery
2	tablespoons minced garlic
2	cups shredded cooked chicken breast
2	cups steamed white rice
2	cups cooked wild rice
1	teaspoon kosher salt
½	teaspoon freshly ground black pepper
¼	teaspoon garlic salt

Cheese Sauce

4	tablespoons (½ stick) butter
¼	cup all-purpose flour
¼	teaspoon salt
¼	teaspoon freshly ground black pepper
2	cups chicken broth
3½	cups shredded cheddar cheese, divided

1. Preheat the oven to 350°F and spray a 9×13-inch baking dish with nonstick cooking spray.

2. Heat the olive oil in a Dutch oven or large pot over medium heat. Add the carrot, onion, and celery and cook, stirring, until tender, about 10 minutes. Add the garlic and cook, stirring, for 1 minute. Add chicken, white and wild rices, salt, pepper, and garlic salt and cook, stirring until hot, about 5 minutes, then reduce the heat to low.

3. To make the cheese sauce, melt the butter in a medium saucepan over medium-high heat. Add the flour, salt, and pepper, whisking to combine. Slowly add the chicken broth, whisking continuously until the liquid thickens and starts to boil. Add 2 cups of the cheese, stirring until melted.

4. Pour the cheese sauce over the rice mixture and stir to combine, then transfer to the prepared baking dish. Top with the remaining 1½ cups cheese and bake for 25 to 30 minutes, until the cheese is melted. Serve immediately.

Makes **6–8** Servings

There is something quite satisfying about making homemade BBQ sauce. I've developed a very simple recipe that is made with everyday ingredients you probably have on hand. Fryer chicken is smothered in my finger-licking sauce, then baked in the oven. The family is in for a treat with this meal. Enjoy with my 3-Cheese and Bacon au Gratin Potatoes (page 48) and a simple salad.

Oven-Baked BBQ Chicken

6	tablespoons packed light brown sugar, divided
1¼	teaspoons kosher salt, divided
2	teaspoons freshly ground black pepper, divided
1	teaspoon smoked paprika
1	teaspoon garlic powder
1	3-pound chicken, cut into 2 wings, 2 breasts, 2 drumsticks, and 2 thighs
1½	cups ketchup
¼	cup Worcestershire sauce
3	tablespoons yellow mustard
2	tablespoons apple cider vinegar
1½	tablespoons fresh lemon juice
2	tablespoons vegetable oil

1. Preheat the oven to 350°F and line a large baking sheet with parchment paper or a silicone liner.

2. Add 2 tablespoons of the brown sugar, 1 teaspoon of the salt, 1 teaspoon of the pepper, the paprika, and the garlic powder to a small bowl and stir to combine. Rub the dry mix on all sides of the chicken pieces.

3. Add the ketchup, Worcestershire sauce, mustard, vinegar, lemon juice, and the remaining 4 tablespoons of brown sugar, ¼ teaspoon salt, and 1 teaspoon pepper to a medium saucepan over medium-low heat and stir to combine. Cook, stirring, for 5 minutes.

4. Heat the oil in a Dutch oven or large pot over medium heat. In batches, add the chicken to the pot and brown for about 3 minutes per side. Transfer the browned chicken pieces to the prepared baking sheet. Add ½ cup of the warm BBQ sauce to a small bowl and brush over both sides of the partially cooked chicken. Bake for 25 to 35 minutes, until the chicken is cooked through. Remove the chicken from the oven, brush with warm BBQ sauce and use any remaining sauce for dipping.

Makes **8** Servings

This is a great chicken dish that is perfect for entertaining or when you just want to impress your family. Fresh garlic brings intense flavor to this dish with the simple marinade I've put together. Everyday ingredients make for a simple and flavorful dinner. Have the kids help prepare the marinade by being in charge of turning the blender on. Once it's ready, they can hold open the zip-top bag the marinade will go into, zip it up, and shake the bag to coat the chicken. Serve with my Creamy Weeknight Mashed Potatoes (page 45) and Parmesan Roasted Carrot Fries (page 50).

Garlic and Caper Marinated Chicken Thighs

2½   pounds chicken thighs
½   cup extra-virgin olive oil
10   cloves garlic
1   teaspoon fresh lemon juice
½   teaspoon dried thyme
½   teaspoon kosher salt
¼   teaspoon freshly ground black pepper
¼   cup capers, drained and rinsed

1. Place the chicken thighs into a large zip-top bag. Add the olive oil, garlic, lemon juice, thyme, salt, and pepper to a blender and blend until smooth. Pour the marinade over the chicken, then add the capers. Massage the chicken with the marinade to mix in the capers. Refrigerate for 4 to 6 hours or overnight.

2. Preheat the oven to 350°F and spray a large baking sheet with nonstick cooking spray.

3. Pour the entire bag of chicken and marinade into the prepared baking sheet, spacing the chicken evenly. Bake for 30 to 35 minutes, until the chicken is cooked through. Let cool for 5 minutes and serve.

Makes
6
Servings

Chicken cutlets are great for weeknight dinners, because they are cut nice and thin, and take only minutes to cook. I developed a blend of my favorite taco seasonings that I sprinkle on both sides of the chicken for a flavor-packed dinner. The kids love to measure out the spices and watch them get mixed together to create a homemade taco seasoning. Serve with my Mini Bean and Cheese Burrito Cups (page 35) and a simple salad.

10-Minute Pan-Fried Chicken Taco Cutlets

¾   teaspoon ground cumin

¾   teaspoon smoked paprika

½   teaspoon kosher salt

½   teaspoon freshly ground black
      pepper

2   pounds chicken cutlets

¼   cup extra-virgin olive oil, divided

1. Add the cumin, paprika, salt, and pepper to a small bowl and stir to combine. Season both sides of the chicken with seasonings, then rub into the chicken with your fingers.

2. Heat 2 tablespoons of the olive oil in a large skillet over medium heat. Add half the chicken to the skillet and cook until cooked through, about 2 minutes per side. Add the remaining 2 tablespoons olive oil and cook the second batch the same way. Transfer the chicken to a serving plate, let rest for 3 to 5 minutes, and serve warm.

Makes
6–8
Servings

I love this recipe because it takes less than 10 minutes to get into the oven. Have the kids toss the vegetables into the roasting dish to help prepare dinner. While the chicken is roasting, you'll be spoiled with a wonderful rosemary and thyme aroma that fills the entire house. When you pull it out of the oven, you've got a gorgeous roasted chicken that looks like you've slaved for hours in the kitchen. Enjoy this meal with a simple salad and my Creamy Honey-Buttered Corn (page 46).

Butter and Herb Whole Roasted Chicken and Vegetables

1	3 to 4 pound whole chicken
4	tablespoons (½ stick) butter, softened
1	teaspoon kosher salt
½	teaspoon freshly ground black pepper
1	teaspoon crushed dried rosemary
1	teaspoon dried thyme
½	cup reduced-sodium chicken broth
2	medium-large russet potatoes, quartered and sliced, about 1-inch pieces
3	large carrots, peeled and cut into 1-inch pieces
4	stalks of celery, cut into 1-inch pieces

1. Preheat the oven to 350°F and spray a roasting pan or 9×13-inch baking dish with nonstick cooking spray.

2. Pat the chicken dry with paper towels. Rub the butter on both sides of the chicken, then season with the salt and pepper. Sprinkle both sides of the chicken with the rosemary and thyme, then place in the prepared baking dish. Pour the chicken broth around the chicken and add the potatoes, carrots, and celery. Bake for 65 to 80 minutes, until chicken is cooked through and the vegetables are tender. Let rest for 10 minutes before carving.

Makes
6
Servings

Put Some Meat on Those Bones

One of the best things about making my Classic Slow-Cooked Pot Roast and Vegetables (page 159) is having leftover roast to make these sandwiches. They seem so simple at first glance, but don't be deceived. After one bite of these juicy sandwiches, you'll be making pot roast on a regular basis. The kids love having their own cup of jus for dipping. The messier, the better, according to them. If you run out of jus, warm some beef broth from a can as a substitute. Serve with Parmesan Roasted Smashed Potatoes (page 49) and steamed vegetables of your choice.

Pot Roast French Dip Sandwiches

2 cups shredded Classic Slow-Cooked Pot Roast (see page 159)

2¼ cups reserved jus from pot roast, divided

8 soft dinner rolls, split

2 cups shredded cheddar cheese

1. Preheat the broiler with a rack placed 5 to 6 inches below the heat source. Heat the shredded pot roast in a medium saucepan with ¼ cup of the reserved jus over medium heat. When hot, reduce the heat to low.

2. Place the rolls split side up onto a large baking sheet. Sprinkle the cheese evenly over the bottom half of each roll, place under the broiler, and bake for 1 to 2 minutes, watching closely so the rolls don't burn, until the cheese is melted and the rolls are toasted. Remove from the oven and place about ¼ cup shredded pot roast over the melted cheese. Close with the top roll and serve with small bowls of the remaining jus for dipping.

Makes **8** Servings

There is something so satisfying about pulling out a homemade lasagna from the oven for dinner. Get the kids involved in helping with all the great layers; they can sprinkle on the cheese and help spread the ricotta on the oven-ready noodles. With just a little prep time, you will have the entire family at your fingertips when they peek inside the oven. Keep in mind that you can always use a premade sauce instead of my homemade one if you are short on time. Enjoy with a simple salad and Cheesy Garlic Toast (page 31) for extra points from the family.

Homemade Creamy Weeknight Lasagna

2	tablespoons extra-virgin olive oil
1	cup finely chopped white onion
1	tablespoon minced garlic
1	pound lean ground beef
¾	teaspoon kosher salt, divided
½	teaspoon freshly ground black pepper, divided
1	28-ounce can crushed tomatoes
¼	cup chopped fresh basil leaves
1	pound part-skim ricotta cheese
2	cups shredded mozzarella cheese, divided
¾	cup freshly grated Parmesan cheese, divided
1	9-ounce box oven-ready lasagna noodles
1	8-ounce package cream cheese, cut into 18 squares

1. Preheat the oven to 350°F and spray a 9×13-inch baking dish with nonstick cooking spray.

2. Heat the oil in a Dutch oven or medium pot over medium heat. Add the onion and cook, stirring, until tender, about 5 minutes. Add the garlic and cook, stirring, for 1 minute. Add the ground beef, ½ teaspoon of the salt, and ¼ teaspoon of the pepper and cook, stirring and breaking up the meat until browned. Drain the fat from the pan if necessary. Add the tomatoes and basil and cook, stirring, until hot, about 5 minutes. Reduce the heat to low and simmer.

3. Add the ricotta, 1 cup of the mozzarella cheese, ½ cup of the Parmesan cheese, and the remaining ¼ teaspoon salt and ¼ teaspoon pepper to a large bowl and mix until well combined.

4. Spoon 1 cup of meat sauce into the prepared baking dish. Place 3 oven-ready lasagna noodles over the sauce. Divide the ricotta mixture into 3 equal parts. Spread one-third of the ricotta evenly over the layer of lasagna noodles. Top evenly with 1 cup meat sauce, then top each noodle with 2 squares of the cream cheese. Repeat this process 2 more times and end with noodles on top (using 12 total lasagna noodles). Top the noodles with the remaining 1 cup meat sauce, then sprinkle the remaining 1 cup mozzarella and ¼ cup Parmesan cheeses over all. Bake for 50 to 60 minutes, until noodles are cooked through. Let sit for 15 minutes before serving.

Makes
8
Servings

I'll never forget an assignment my oldest son had in kindergarten that asked what his favorite food was. He immediately yelled out "Meatballs," then asked me how to spell while writing down the letters as fast as his little kindergartner fingers could write. Prepare yourself for juicy meatballs stuffed with oozing mozzarella that are beautifully nestled in a simple pasta sauce over spaghetti, eaten on a fork if you are my 9-year-old, or layered inside a soft baguette smothered in melted cheese and pasta sauce.

Momma's Homemade Mozzarella-Stuffed Meatballs

2	tablespoons extra-virgin olive oil
1	pound lean ground beef
1	large egg
½	cup finely chopped white onion
½	cup Japanese panko bread crumbs
½	cup freshly grated Parmesan cheese
¼	cup milk
2	tablespoons minced garlic
1	tablespoon Worcestershire sauce
1	tablespoon yellow mustard
1	teaspoon hot sauce, like Tabasco
½	teaspoon kosher salt
¼	teaspoon freshly ground black pepper
¼	teaspoon garlic salt
12	to 14 1-inch fresh mozzarella balls

1. Preheat the oven to 350°F and grease a 9×13-inch baking dish with the olive oil.

2. Add the beef, egg, onion, bread crumbs, Parmesan cheese, milk, garlic, Worcestershire sauce, mustard, hot sauce, salt, pepper, and garlic salt to a large mixing bowl and stir until just combined. Take ¼ cup beef mixture and press an indentation into the center with your thumb to make room for the cheese. Place a cheese ball into the indentation, then with your hands, enclose the cheese with the beef mixture, making sure the cheese is completely enclosed. Place meatballs into the prepared baking dish and bake for 30 to 35 minutes, until browned and cooked through.

Makes **12–14** Servings

Sloppy Joes are family friendly, messy, and absolutely necessary from time to time. I've developed a simple, sweet, and chunky meat sauce that is irresistible inside soft rolls. Have the kids help measure out the vegetables and add them to the pot. Serve with Parmesan Roasted Smashed Potatoes (page 49) and a simple salad.

Homemade Sloppy Joes

2	tablespoons extra-virgin olive oil
1	cup finely chopped white onion
¾	cup diced celery
¾	cup diced carrot
¼	cup chopped mini sweet peppers
1	tablespoon minced garlic
1	pound lean ground beef
¾	teaspoon kosher salt, divided
¼	teaspoon freshly ground black pepper
1	cup ketchup
1½	tablespoons yellow mustard
1	tablespoon Worcestershire sauce
¾	teaspoon chili powder
8	soft Kaiser rolls, split

1. Heat the olive oil in a Dutch oven or medium pot over medium heat. Add the onion, celery, carrot, and peppers and cook, stirring, until tender, about 10 minutes. Add the garlic and cook, stirring, for 1 minute. Add the ground beef, ½ teaspoon of the salt, and the pepper and cook, stirring and breaking up meat until browned. Drain the fat from the pan if necessary. Reduce the heat to low.

2. Add the ketchup, mustard, Worcestershire sauce, chili powder, and the remaining ¼ teaspoon salt to a medium bowl and stir to combine. Add the sauce to the beef mixture, stirring until well combined. Reduce the heat to low and simmer.

3. Spoon the warm meat mixture inside the split rolls and serve.

Makes
8
Servings

If you couldn't tell from reading my blog, I love having fun with dinner, like this spaghetti pot pie. I top two pie plates of spaghetti with refrigerated pie crust that is lightly brushed with olive oil and seasoned with garlic salt. You are eating your garlic toast right along with your spaghetti in one plate. The kids get a kick out of seeing spaghetti in a different form and love the flaky garlic crust pieces. Serve with a simple salad, and you are good to go.

Garlic-Toasted Spaghetti Pot Pie

1	pound thin spaghetti
2	tablespoons plus 1 teaspoon extra-virgin olive oil
1	cup finely chopped white onion
1	tablespoon minced garlic
1	pound lean ground beef
1	28-ounce can crushed tomatoes
¼	cup chopped fresh basil leaves
¾	teaspoon kosher salt
¾	teaspoon garlic salt, divided
½	teaspoon granulated sugar
¼	teaspoon freshly ground black pepper
¼	teaspoon Italian seasoning
½	cup freshly grated Parmesan cheese
2	refrigerated 9-inch pie crusts

1. Preheat the oven to 350°F and spray two 9-inch deep-dish pie plates with nonstick cooking spray.

2. Cook the spaghetti according to the package directions and drain.

3. While pasta is cooking, heat 2 tablespoons of the olive oil in a large Dutch oven or pot over medium heat. Add the onion and cook, stirring, until tender, about 5 minutes. Add the garlic and cook, stirring, for 1 minute. Add the beef and cook, stirring and breaking up the meat until browned. Drain the fat from the pan if necessary. Add the tomatoes, basil, salt, ¼ teaspoon of the garlic salt, the sugar, pepper, and Italian seasoning. Reduce the heat to low and add the cooked pasta to the pot, stirring to combine.

4. Divide the spaghetti mixture between the prepared pie plates. Top each with ¼ cup of the Parmesan cheese, then top with the pie crusts and crimp the edges. Brush each pie top with remaining 1 teaspoon olive oil and season with remaining ½ teaspoon garlic salt. Bake for 30 to 35 minutes, until pie crust is golden brown. Let cool for 5 minutes before serving.

Makes **8** Servings

These baby cheeseburgers may be tiny in size, but they are a massive hit in our home. They are quick enough to prepare for busy weeknights and perfect for parties too. I developed a simple "special sauce" that reminds me of the sauce that restaurants add to their burgers. Have fun experimenting with toppings—add your favorites. I cook these burgers right on the stovetop, but they are great prepared on the grill too. If mini burgers are not your thing, make 4 regular-size burgers instead.

Pan-Fried Baby Bacon Cheeseburgers with Special Sauce

1	pound lean ground beef
¾	cup finely chopped white onion
2	tablespoons minced garlic
1	tablespoon Worcestershire sauce
½	teaspoon kosher salt
¼	teaspoon freshly ground black pepper
¼	teaspoon garlic salt
2	tablespoons extra-virgin olive oil
4	slices cheddar cheese, each cut in half
8	soft dinner-size rolls, split
½	cup mayonnaise
2	tablespoons ketchup
2	tablespoons dill pickle relish
1	cup baby spinach leaves
8	slices tomato
8	strips bacon, cooked until crisp
16	slices dill pickle

1. Add the beef, onion, garlic, Worcestershire sauce, salt, pepper, and garlic salt to a large mixing bowl and mix until just combined. Form into eight 3-inch patties, about ½ inch thick.

2. Heat the olive oil in a large skillet over medium heat. In two batches, add the burgers to the skillet and cook until browned and cooked through, about 3 minutes on each side. After flipping, place a half slice of cheese over each burger to melt. Transfer the cooked burgers to a plate to rest for 3 to 5 minutes.

3. Place the rolls cut side down in the same skillet and toast until lightly browned, about 2 minutes. Add the mayonnaise, ketchup, and relish to a small bowl and mix to combine. Spread on the toasted rolls. Layer the bottom roll with a few spinach leaves, 1 burger, 1 tomato slice, 1 strip of bacon broken in half, and 2 pickle slices. Close with the top roll and serve.

Makes
8
Servings

Reed is my all-star father-in-law, who is not only a cool guy, great dad and grandpa, but also an incredible cook. He makes delicious family-style meals for his large family and does it well. I've always been a fan of Reed's quick and easy Mexican-style meals that are full of flavor without too much time spent in the kitchen. His Beef Enchilada Bake fits the bill perfectly. Enjoy with Spanish Rice (page 51) or Southwest Quinoa Salad (page 57) and a simple salad.

Reed's Beef Enchilada Bake

2	tablespoons extra-virgin olive oil
1	pound lean ground beef
1	teaspoon kosher salt
1	teaspoon ground cumin
½	teaspoon freshly ground black pepper
¼	teaspoon garlic salt
1	15-ounce can red enchilada sauce
1	14.5-ounce can diced tomatoes
1	10.75-ounce can cream of chicken soup
1	10.75-ounce can cheddar cheese soup
1	6-ounce can small black olives, chopped
12	corn tortillas
2	cups shredded cheddar cheese

1. Preheat the oven to 350°F and spray a 9×13-inch baking dish with nonstick cooking spray.

2. Heat the olive oil in a Dutch oven or large pot over medium heat. Add the beef, salt, cumin, pepper, and garlic salt and cook, stirring and breaking up the meat until browned, 5 to 7 minutes. Drain the fat from the pan if necessary. Add the enchilada sauce, tomatoes, cream of chicken soup, cheese soup, and black olives and stir to combine.

3. Break up the tortillas into 1-inch pieces, add to the pot and stir to combine. Transfer to the prepared baking dish and sprinkle with the cheddar cheese. Bake for 25 to 30 minutes, until cheese is melted.

Makes
8–10
Servings

Meatloaf is one of those comfort foods that make you happy and warm inside. It reminds me of eating at Granna's house and enjoying meatloaf sandwiches lathered in mayonnaise. I've developed my own flavor-packed meatloaf with a homemade BBQ-peach glaze that is brushed on top before baking. Enjoy with Creamy Weeknight Mashed Potatoes (page 45) and Creamy Honey-Buttered Corn (page 46).

BBQ-Peach-Glazed Meatloaf

1	pound lean ground beef
2	large eggs
1	cup finely chopped white onion
¾	cup Japanese panko bread crumbs
¼	cup chopped fresh parsley
2	tablespoons milk
1	tablespoon yellow mustard
1	tablespoon minced garlic
½	teaspoon kosher salt
¼	teaspoon freshly ground black pepper
¼	teaspoon garlic salt
2	1-inch-thick slices fresh, frozen, or canned peaches
2	tablespoons prepared BBQ sauce

1. Preheat the oven to 350°F and spray a large baking sheet with nonstick cooking spray.

2. Add the beef, eggs, onion, bread crumbs, parsley, milk, mustard, garlic, salt, pepper, and garlic salt to a large bowl and mix with hands or a spoon until combined. Transfer to a prepared baking sheet and form into a 4×10-inch oval.

3. Add the peach slices to a blender or food processor and blend until smooth. Add the BBQ sauce and peach purée to a small bowl and mix until combined.

4. Brush the sauce over the meatloaf and bake for 30 to 35 minutes, until cooked through. Let cool for 5 minutes and cut into slices.

Makes **8** Servings

This recipe has Sunday dinner written all over it. I came to find out, shepherd's pie is traditionally prepared with ground lamb, but since I grew up enjoying it with ground beef that is the version I prepare. My father-in-law, Reed, makes a great shepherd's pie with a tomato-based beef layer, and my mom makes her version with a creamy beef layer that my boys would give up their favorite toys for. I've developed my own version that has won the hearts of many. I love watching my boys do a happy dance every time word gets out that Mom is making this dish.

Home-Style Shepherd's Pie

2½	pounds russet potatoes, peeled and diced
6	tablespoons (¾ stick) unsalted butter, divided
1¼	teaspoon kosher salt, divided
¾	teaspoon freshly ground black pepper, divided
¼	teaspoon garlic salt
1	cup milk
2	tablespoons extra-virgin olive oil
1	cup finely chopped white onion
1	tablespoon minced garlic
1	pound lean ground beef
1	15-ounce can green beans, drained and rinsed
3	tablespoons all-purpose flour
1	cup reduced-sodium chicken broth
1	cup shredded cheddar cheese

1. Preheat the oven to 350°F and spray a 9×13-inch baking dish with nonstick cooking spray.

2. Add the diced potatoes to a Dutch oven or large pot with water. Bring the water to a boil and boil until the potatoes are fork tender, 13 to 15 minutes. Drain and transfer the potatoes to the bowl of a stand mixer. With the mixer on low, beat in 3 tablespoons of the butter, ½ teaspoon of the salt, ¼ teaspoon of the pepper, and the garlic salt. Slowly add the milk, mixing until creamy.

3. Heat the olive oil in a large skillet over medium heat. Add the onion and cook, stirring, until tender, about 5 minutes. Add the garlic and cook, stirring, for 1 minute. Add the beef, ½ teaspoon of the remaining salt, and ¼ teaspoon of the remaining pepper and cook, stirring and breaking up the meat until browned. Drain the fat from the pan if necessary. Add the green beans, stir to combine, and reduce the heat to low.

4. Melt the remaining 3 tablespoons butter in a medium saucepan over medium heat. Add the flour and the remaining ¼ teaspoon salt and ¼ teaspoon pepper, whisking until combined. Slowly add the chicken broth, whisking until thick and creamy. Add the sauce to the meat mixture, stirring, then transfer the mixture to the prepared baking dish. Top with the mashed potatoes, then sprinkle with the shredded cheese. Bake for 20 to 25 minutes, until cheese is melted through.

Makes **8** Servings

This is a no-fuss dinner that will get you in and out of the kitchen in no time. I've developed a speedy meat sauce that is tossed with rigatoni and covered in mozzarella and Parmesan cheeses cooked right on the stovetop. The family will love this Italian-style pasta dish that is perfect with Cheesy Garlic Toast (page 31) and a simple salad.

Rigatoni Skillet Dinner

8	ounces dry rigatoni
2	tablespoons extra-virgin olive oil
1	cup finely chopped white onion
2	tablespoons minced garlic
1	pound lean ground beef
¾	teaspoon kosher salt
¼	teaspoon freshly ground black pepper
¼	teaspoon garlic salt
¼	teaspoon Italian seasoning
1	28-ounce can crushed tomatoes
¼	cup shredded Parmesan cheese
1	cup shredded mozzarella cheese

1. Cook the pasta according to the package directions, drain, and run under cold water to stop the cooking.

2. Heat the olive oil in a Dutch oven or large pot over medium heat. Add the onion and cook, stirring, until tender, about 5 minutes. Add the garlic and cook, stirring, for 1 minute. Add the beef, salt, pepper, garlic salt, and Italian seasoning and cook, stirring and breaking up the meat until browned, 5 to 7 minutes. Drain the fat from pan if necessary. Add the tomatoes, Parmesan cheese, and cooked pasta and stir to combine. Reduce the heat to low, top with the mozzarella cheese, and cover with the lid to melt, about 5 minutes. Remove the lid and serve.

Makes
6–8
Servings

It's a good thing this recipe makes two large pans because these shells go quick. Grab some spoons and have the whole family help stuff shells to get dinner in the oven in no time. While the shells are baking, prepare a simple salad and Cheesy Garlic Toast (page 31). Since this recipe makes large servings, enjoy one dish for dinner and give the other to a friend who might be in need, or freeze one to enjoy later.

Italian Sausage–Stuffed Shells

2   1-pound boxes jumbo pasta shells

2   tablespoons extra-virgin olive oil

1   pound sweet Italian sausage

2   28-ounce cans crushed tomatoes

½   teaspoon red pepper flakes

½   teaspoon kosher salt, divided

½   teaspoon freshly ground black pepper, divided

2   15-ounce containers ricotta cheese

1   cup freshly grated Parmesan cheese

3   cups shredded mozzarella cheese, divided

1. Preheat the oven to 350°F and spray two 9×13-inch baking dishes and a large skillet with nonstick cooking spray.

2. Cook the pasta shells according to the package directions, drain, and brush the shells lightly with the olive oil to keep from sticking.

3. Heat the prepared skillet over medium heat. Add the sausage and cook, stirring and breaking up the meat until browned, 5 to 7 minutes. Drain the fat from the pan if necessary. Add the crushed tomatoes, red pepper flakes, ¼ teaspoon of the salt, and ¼ teaspoon of the pepper and stir to combine. Reduce the heat to low and simmer.

4. Add the ricotta, Parmesan cheese, 1 cup of the mozzarella, and the remaining ¼ teaspoon salt and ¼ teaspoon pepper to a large mixing bowl and mix to combine.

5. Spoon ½ cup of meat sauce into the bottom of each of the prepared baking dishes. Spoon 2 tablespoons of the ricotta filling into each cooked shell, then place the shells seam side down in the prepared baking dishes. Top both dishes of shells evenly with the sauce and the remaining 2 cups shredded mozzarella. Bake for 25 to 30 minutes, until the cheese is bubbly and melted.

Makes
12
Servings

Pork tenderloin is such a simple and satisfying dinner. With my sweet and smoky rub, you'll have dinner in the oven in about 5 minutes. The kids love digging into my cooking utensil drawer to grab the teaspoons so they can help measure out the spices for the rub. Be sure to let your tenderloin rest for a good 10 minutes before slicing; this will ensure juicier pieces of pork. Enjoy this dish with Creamy Honey-Buttered Corn (page 46), Creamy Weeknight Mashed Potatoes (page 45), and a simple salad.

Sweet and Smoky Pork Tenderloin

3	tablespoons packed light brown sugar
1	teaspoon smoked paprika
1	teaspoon kosher salt
½	teaspoon freshly ground black pepper
¼	teaspoon garlic salt
¼	teaspoon ground cumin
1	pound pork tenderloin

1. Preheat the oven to 350°F and line a medium baking sheet with parchment paper.

2. Add the brown sugar, paprika, salt, pepper, garlic salt, and cumin to a small bowl and stir to combine. Rub the seasoning mixture all over the pork tenderloin.

3. Transfer the pork to the prepared baking sheet and bake for 33 to 40 minutes, until cooked through. Let rest for 10 minutes before slicing.

Makes
6
Servings

Gone Fishin'

Shrimp scampi is a simple and flavorful way to enjoy shrimp. Butter, lemon, and garlic make for a zesty sauce for this simple dinner. There are many ways you can buy shrimp—fresh or frozen, with or without tails, peeled or unpeeled, deveined and not deveined. I generally buy fresh or frozen that is peeled and deveined. This makes life a little easier when preparing dinner. Have the kids help measure out the onions and add them to the pot with the shrimp. Serve with a simple salad.

Simple Shrimp Scampi

1	pound linguini
7	tablespoons unsalted butter, divided
2	tablespoons extra-virgin olive oil
½	cup finely chopped white onion
4	cloves garlic, minced
1½	pounds medium raw shrimp, peeled and deveined
¼	teaspoon kosher salt
¼	teaspoon freshly ground black pepper
½	cup reduced-sodium chicken broth
2	tablespoons fresh lemon juice
¼	cup chopped fresh parsley
¼	cup chopped fresh chives

1. Cook the linguini according to the package directions, drain, and run under cool water to stop the cooking.

2. Heat 5 tablespoons of the butter and the olive oil in a Dutch oven or large pot over medium heat. Add the onion and cook, stirring, until tender, 3 to 5 minutes. Add the garlic and cook, stirring, for 1 minute. Add the shrimp, salt, and pepper and cook, stirring, until hot, 4 to 6 minutes. Add the chicken broth and lemon juice and stir to combine. Add the parsley, chives, and the remaining 2 tablespoons butter and stir to combine. Spoon the shrimp and sauce over the linguini. Serve immediately.

Makes **6** Servings

Tilapia is a great fish to start the family with if they are afraid of seafood. It is mild in taste, white, and lean. The kids enjoy the marinara and oozing mozzarella cheese over each piece of tilapia. This simple recipe takes just minutes to get into the oven and is great served with my Cheesy Garlic Toast (page 31) and a simple salad.

Baked Tilapia Parmesan

4	tilapia fillets
¾	teaspoon kosher salt
½	teaspoon freshly ground black pepper
½	cup shredded Parmesan cheese
8	large fresh basil leaves
1	15-ounce can crushed tomatoes
1	cup shredded mozzarella cheese

1. Preheat the oven to 350°F and spray a 9×13-inch baking dish with nonstick cooking spray.

2. Season both sides of the tilapia with the salt and pepper and place in the prepared baking dish. Layer with the Parmesan cheese, basil, tomatoes, and mozzarella cheese. Bake for 25 to 30 minutes, until the tilapia flakes easily with a fork.

Makes
4
Servings

These tilapia tacos are packed with my favorite Mexican seasonings and topped with a creamy cilantro sauce. Tilapia cooks quickly, so you'll have dinner on the table in about 15 minutes. Have the kids help set out all of the toppings for the tacos. Enjoy with my Spanish Rice (page 51).

Tilapia Tacos with Cilantro-Cream Sauce and Avocado

1	teaspoon extra-virgin olive oil
1	tablespoon plus ½ teaspoon fresh lime juice
¼	teaspoon ground cumin
½	teaspoon kosher salt, divided
½	teaspoon freshly ground black pepper, divided
¼	teaspoon garlic salt
4	tilapia fillets (1 to 1½ pounds)
4	ounces sour cream
½	cup chopped fresh cilantro leaves
¼	teaspoon hot sauce, like Tabasco
8	corn tortillas or soft tortilla bread
2	cups shredded white cabbage
2	large avocados, peeled, pitted, and diced into ½-inch pieces

1. Heat the olive oil in a large skillet over medium heat. Add 1 tablespoon of the lime juice and swirl to coat the pan.

2. Add the cumin, ¼ teaspoon of the salt, ¼ teaspoon of the pepper, and the garlic salt to a small bowl, mix to combine, and rub over both sides of the tilapia fillets. In batches, place the tilapia in the skillet and cook until the fish flakes easily with a fork, 3 to 4 minutes per side.

3. To make the sauce, add the sour cream, cilantro, hot sauce, and the remaining ½ teaspoon lime juice, ¼ teaspoon salt, and ¼ teaspoon pepper in a medium bowl and stir to combine.

4. With 2 forks, shred the fish into bite-size pieces. Divide the fish among the tortillas, top with shredded cabbage, and drizzle with the cilantro-cream sauce. Top with the avocado and serve.

Makes **8** Servings

This creamy tomato and shrimp linguini dinner is a great weeknight meal that can be prepared in under 30 minutes with a few basic ingredients that you are likely to have on hand. You'll be in and out of the kitchen in no time. The kids love to be in charge of turning on the food processor or blender for the tomato cream sauce. Serve with a simple salad and my Cheesy Garlic Toast (page 31).

Shrimp Linguini in Tomato Cream Sauce

1	pound linguini
2	tablespoons extra-virgin olive oil
1	pound medium raw shrimp, peeled and deveined
¾	teaspoon kosher salt, divided
½	teaspoon freshly ground black pepper, divided
1	28-ounce can crushed tomatoes
¼	cup chopped white onion
1	clove garlic
5	large fresh basil leaves
¼	cup heavy cream

1. Cook the linguini according to the package directions, drain, and run under cool water to stop the cooking.

2. Heat the olive oil in a Dutch oven or medium pot over medium heat. Add the shrimp, ½ teaspoon of the salt, and ¼ teaspoon of the pepper and cook, stirring, for 5 minutes. Reduce the heat to low.

3. Add the tomatoes, onion, garlic, basil, and the remaining ¼ teaspoon salt and ¼ teaspoon pepper to a food processor or blender. Pulse until smooth. Add to the shrimp and stir to combine. Add the heavy cream, stir to combine, and cook until hot, about 5 minutes. Serve the linguini with spoonfuls of the shrimp in tomato cream sauce.

Makes **6** Servings

These quick-to-prepare shrimp skewers are brushed with a zesty lime dressing that is served over a simple brown butter and garlic quinoa. Quinoa is usually considered a whole grain but is actually a seed that can be prepared as a whole grain. It is so nice because it cooks in just 10 to 15 minutes. Quinoa is a great substitute for rice. This flavor-packed dinner is ready in about 20 minutes, which is perfect for busy weeknights. Enjoy with a simple salad and my Creamy Honey-Buttered Corn (page 46).

Chili-Lime Shrimp Skewers over Garlic Butter Quinoa

1	cup quinoa
16	medium raw shrimp, peeled and deveined
4	wooden skewers
1	tablespoon plus ¼ teaspoon fresh lime juice
¾	teaspoon plus ⅛ teaspoon chili powder
¾	teaspoon kosher salt, divided
½	teaspoon freshly ground black pepper, divided
5	tablespoons butter, divided
1	clove garlic, minced
¼	teaspoon garlic salt

1. Rinse the quinoa in warm water. Bring 2 cups of water to a boil in a 2-quart saucepan. Add the quinoa, bring back to a boil, cover, and cook over medium heat until water is absorbed, 12 minutes. Remove from heat, fluff, and let stand for 15 minutes.

2. Heat a grill or grill pan to medium heat. Grease the grill with oil or spray the grill pan with nonstick cooking spray.

3. Place 4 shrimp onto each of 4 skewers and brush both sides with 1 tablespoon of the lime juice. Add ¾ teaspoon of the chili powder, ¼ teaspoon of the salt, and ¼ teaspoon of the pepper to a small bowl and mix to combine. Season both sides of the shrimp with the chili-salt. Place the skewers on the grill or grill pan and cook until heated through, about 3 minutes per side. Add 2 tablespoons of the butter to a microwave-safe bowl and microwave until melted, about 15 seconds. Add the remaining ¼ teaspoon lime juice and ⅛ teaspoon chili powder, stir to combine, and brush over the shrimp.

4. Add the remaining 3 tablespoons butter to a small skillet over medium heat, swirling until melted. Add the garlic and cook, stirring, for 1 minute. Pour over the cooked quinoa, stir to combine, and season with the remaining ½ teaspoon salt and ¼ teaspoon pepper and the garlic salt. Mix to combine. Transfer the quinoa to a large serving plate and top with shrimp skewers.

Makes 4 Servings

This simple yet impressive salmon dish has those irresistible sweet and smoky flavor combinations going on. The salmon is lightly seasoned with a smoky rub, then brushed with sweet maple syrup, and baked in under 20 minutes. My boys love to help measure out the spices for the rub, place them in a bowl, and stir. I serve the fish on top of a bed of garlic corn with a simple salad.

Smoky Maple-Baked Salmon over Garlic Corn

1	teaspoon kosher salt, divided
¾	teaspoon freshly ground pepper, divided
¾	teaspoon smoked paprika
4	salmon fillets (1½ to 2 pounds)
2	tablespoons pure maple syrup
2	tablespoons extra-virgin olive oil
2	cloves garlic, minced
2	cups fresh or frozen corn kernels
2	tablespoons finely chopped fresh cilantro

1. Preheat the oven to 450°F and line a medium baking sheet with parchment paper.

2. Add ¾ teaspoon of the salt, ½ teaspoon of the pepper, and the paprika to a small bowl and mix to combine. Season both sides of the salmon fillets with the rub and place on the baking sheet. Brush the maple syrup over the tops of the fillets and bake for 12 to 15 minutes, until the fish flakes easily with a fork and is cooked through.

3. Heat the olive oil in a large skillet over medium heat. Add the garlic and cook, stirring, for 1 minute. Add the corn, cilantro, and the remaining ¼ teaspoon salt and ¼ teaspoon pepper and cook, stirring, until hot, about 3 minutes. Serve each plate with ½ cup of the corn and a piece of salmon on top.

Makes
4
Servings

Brace yourself for a giant salmon burger. This one is layered with the works. I love how fast fish cooks, which means you'll have dinner on the table in no time at all. This is a great recipe to have the kids help do the mixing. My boys love to lean on the counter and pick their favorite spoon from my kitchen utensils. Mixing lemon and dill with the mayonnaise gives the perfect punch of flavor to each bite. Serve with a simple salad.

Salmon Burgers with Lemon-Dill Mayonnaise

4	salmon fillets (1 to 1½ pounds)
1	teaspoon kosher salt, divided
1	teaspoon freshly ground black pepper, divided
2	large eggs
1	cup Japanese panko bread crumbs
¼	cup chopped fresh parsley
¼	cup buttermilk
3	tablespoons minced garlic
3	tablespoons fresh lemon juice, divided
½	cup mayonnaise
½	teaspoon dried dill weed
2	tablespoons extra-virgin olive oil
6	hamburger-size rolls, split
6	large lettuce leaves
6	slices tomato, ¼ inch thick

1. Preheat the oven to 450°F and line a medium baking sheet with parchment paper.

2. Season both sides of the salmon with ½ teaspoon of the salt and ¼ teaspoon of the pepper. Bake for 12 to 15 minutes, until the fish flakes easily with a fork and is cooked through. Let cool for 10 minutes, then shred the salmon with two forks. Add the shredded salmon to a large bowl.

3. Add the eggs, bread crumbs, parsley, buttermilk, garlic, 2 tablespoons of the lemon juice, the remaining ½ teaspoon salt, and ½ teaspoon of the remaining pepper to the bowl with the salmon and stir until well combined. Form into 6 equal-size patties.

4. Add the mayonnaise, dill, and the remaining ¼ teaspoon pepper and 1 tablespoon lemon juice to a small bowl and mix to combine.

5. Heat the olive oil in a large skillet over medium heat. In batches, add the salmon patties and cook, until golden brown, 3 to 5 minutes per side.

6. In batches, toast the rolls, cut side down, in the same skillet over medium heat for 1 to 2 minutes. Remove and spread the rolls with the lemon-dill mayonnaise and layer the bottoms of the rolls with 1 lettuce leaf, 1 salmon burger, and 1 tomato slice. Close with top rolls and serve.

Makes
6
Servings

There is a restaurant in Arizona we visit often that serves the best shrimp mango quesadillas. They are creamy, cheesy, and full of diced shrimp and mango. I developed my own version of this restaurant favorite that is equally delicious. The boys love the sweet, juicy mango pieces, and the cheesy stuffed buttery crisp tortillas are hard to resist. Enjoy with my Spanish Rice (page 51) and Teedo's Famous Salsa (page 33).

Shrimp-Mango Quesadillas

2	tablespoons extra-virgin olive oil
½	pound medium raw shrimp, peeled, deveined, and tails removed
¾	teaspoon kosher salt, divided
½	teaspoon freshly ground black pepper, divided
6	ounces cream cheese, softened
1	cup shredded cheddar cheese
¼	cup chopped fresh cilantro leaves
4	tablespoons (½ stick) unsalted butter, softened, divided
4	burrito-size (10-inch) flour tortillas
1	cup chopped mango, divided

1. Heat the olive oil in a large skillet over medium heat. Add the shrimp, ½ teaspoon of the salt, and ¼ teaspoon of the pepper, and cook, stirring, for 5 minutes. Remove from the heat.

2. Add the cream cheese, cheddar cheese, cilantro, and the remaining ¼ teaspoon salt and ¼ teaspoon pepper to a medium bowl and stir until well combined.

3. Heat a separate large skillet over medium heat. Spread 1 tablespoon of the butter on one side of a tortilla and place the tortilla buttered side down in the skillet. Spread ¼ cup of the cheese spread over the top of the tortilla. Top with ¼ cup of the cooked shrimp and ¼ cup of the chopped mango on half of the tortilla. With a spatula, fold the tortilla in half, cooking until golden brown, 2 to 3 minutes on each side. Remove from the skillet and cut the quesadillas into wedges to serve. Repeat with the remaining ingredients.

Makes
4
Servings

Chapter 7

You'll Never Miss the Beef

You won't even know these quesadillas are meatless, with all of the vegetables and cheeses stuffed inside each tortilla. They are buttery crisp on the outside while cheesy and creamy on the inside. Have the kids help measure out the zucchini and cheese. My boys love watching the cheese ooze out the sides of each quesadilla. Serve with my Mini Bean and Cheese Burrito Cups (page 35) and Spanish Rice (page 51).

Veggie Quesadillas with Cilantro Cream

4 ounces cream cheese, softened

¼ cup chopped fresh cilantro

½ teaspoon kosher salt, divided

½ teaspoon freshly ground black
   pepper, divided

2 tablespoons extra-virgin olive oil

1 cup thinly sliced zucchini

¾ cup grape tomatoes, sliced
   lengthwise

1 cup finely chopped white onion

1 tablespoon minced garlic

4 tablespoons (½ stick) butter,
   softened, divided

4 10-inch flour tortillas

1 cup shredded cheddar cheese,
   divided

1. Add the cream cheese, cilantro, ¼ teaspoon of the salt, and ¼ teaspoon of the pepper to a medium bowl and stir to combine.

2. Heat the olive oil in a 12-inch skillet over medium heat. Add the zucchini, tomatoes, onion, garlic, and the remaining ¼ teaspoon salt and ¼ teaspoon pepper and cook, stirring, until tender, about 5 minutes. Remove from the heat and transfer to a medium bowl.

3. Wipe the skillet clean with a paper towel, spray with nonstick cooking spray, and place over medium heat. Spread 1 tablespoon of the butter on one side of a tortilla and place buttered side down in the hot skillet. Spread 2 tablespoons of the cilantro cream over half of the tortilla, then place ¼ cup cooked vegetables on the other half. Top the vegetable side of the quesadilla with ¼ cup of the cheddar cheese, then fold the tortilla in half, pressing the cilantro cream into the vegetable side. Cook until both sides of the tortilla are browned, about 2 minutes each side. Continue cooking the remaining quesadillas in the same manner.

4. Cut each quesadilla into 4 wedges and serve warm.

Makes
4
Servings

There is something so comforting about a homemade pasta sauce. I will be the first to admit I always have a good jar of pasta sauce on hand for busy weeknights, but it is so great to have a homemade sauce to serve over your favorite noodles. The buttery, cheesy wagon wheels magically take the kids' minds off all of the veggies inside the pasta sauce. Serve with a simple salad and Cheesy Garlic Toast (page 31).

15-Minute Homemade Pasta Sauce over Buttered Wagon Wheels

2	tablespoons extra-virgin olive oil
1	cup finely chopped white onion
1	cup chopped zucchini
1	cup chopped fresh spinach leaves
¼	cup finely chopped mini sweet peppers
1	tablespoon minced garlic
1	28-ounce can crushed tomatoes
¼	cup chopped fresh basil leaves
¾	teaspoon kosher salt
½	teaspoon granulated sugar
¼	teaspoon fresh cracked black pepper
¼	teaspoon garlic salt
¼	teaspoon Italian seasoning
1	pound wagon wheel pasta
4	tablespoons (½ stick) butter
½	teaspoon garlic salt
½	cup shredded Parmesan cheese

1. Heat the olive oil in a Dutch oven or large pot over medium heat. Add the onion, zucchini, spinach, and peppers and cook, stirring, until tender, 8 to 10 minutes. Add the garlic and cook, stirring, for 1 minute. Add the crushed tomatoes, basil, salt, sugar, pepper, garlic salt, and Italian seasoning and stir to combine. Reduce the heat to low and let simmer, about 10 minutes.

2. Cook the pasta according to the package directions. Drain and return to the pot. Add the butter, garlic salt, and Parmesan cheese and stir to combine. Serve with the pasta sauce.

Makes
6–8
Servings

My sister and I had the privilege of living walking distance from a large mall in our sunny Arizona neighborhood growing up. I have the best memories of sprinting to the mall in our pre-teen years and living it up at the movie theater, arcade room, and the food court. One of our favorite places was a pizza shop, where I would consistently order their stuffed pizza pie. I created a similar version to the one I had so many times as a teenybopper. Stuff your pie with your favorite pizza toppings—sky's the limit.

Ricotta-Stuffed Spinach and Broccoli Pizza Pie

2	cups fresh broccoli florets
1	pound refrigerated pizza dough
1	cup ricotta cheese
¼	cup freshly grated Parmesan cheese
2	tablespoons extra-virgin olive oil, divided
2	cups chopped fresh spinach leaves
¼	teaspoon kosher salt
¼	teaspoon freshly ground black pepper
½	cup prepared roasted red bell peppers
1½	cups shredded mozzarella cheese
½	teaspoon dried Italian seasoning

1. Preheat the oven to 375°F and spray a 9-inch cake pan with nonstick cooking spray.

2. Bring a Dutch oven or large pot three-fourths full of water over high heat to boil. Add the broccoli and boil until fork tender, about 3 minutes. Drain and set aside.

3. Divide the dough into 2 equal pieces. Spread and press one half of the dough in the bottom and up the sides of the prepared cake pan.

4. Add the ricotta and Parmesan cheeses to a large bowl and stir to combine. Spread onto the pressed pizza dough in the cake pan.

5. Heat 1 tablespoon of the olive oil in a medium skillet over medium heat. Add the spinach and cook, stirring, until wilted, about 5 minutes. Spread evenly over the ricotta cheese layer. Top with the cooked broccoli and season with the salt and pepper. Layer with the roasted peppers and mozzarella cheese.

6. Press out the remaining piece of dough with your hands or a rolling pin and drape over the filling, tucking the edges inside of the pan. Brush with the remaining 1 tablespoon olive oil and sprinkle with Italian seasoning. Bake for 30 to 35 minutes, until the crust is golden brown and cooked through. Let cool for 10 minutes before removing from the pan and cutting into wedges.

Makes **8** Servings

We love rice around our home and often enjoy it as a main dish. This recipe is packed with gorgeous vegetables and is seasoned nicely with Parmesan cheese. When you are serving a dish that is packed with colorful vegetables, challenge the kids to see who can eat the most colors of the rainbow on their plate. A little competition always seems to work for us. Serve with a simple salad.

Parmesan-Vegetable Rice Florentine

2	cups long-grain white rice
2	tablespoons extra-virgin olive oil
1¼	cups finely chopped white onion
½	cup chopped mini sweet peppers
2	tablespoons minced garlic
1	10-ounce bag chopped spinach leaves
½	cup shredded Parmesan cheese
1	teaspoon kosher salt
¼	teaspoon freshly ground black pepper

1. Bring a large saucepan with 2 cups of water to boil. Stir in rice, cover, and reduce heat to low. Simmer for 20 minutes, until the water is absorbed. Set aside.

2. Heat the olive oil in a Dutch oven or large pot over medium heat. Add the onion and sweet peppers and cook, stirring, until tender, about 5 minutes. Add the garlic and cook, stirring, for 1 minute. Add the spinach and cook, stirring, until wilted, about 5 minutes. Add the Parmesan cheese, salt, pepper, and cooked rice and cook, stirring, until heated through, about 5 minutes. Reduce the heat to low and serve.

Makes
8
Servings

This hearty, vegetable-packed chili makes for a perfect dinner any night of the week. Slice and chop all of your vegetables in advance and have the kids help by adding them to the big pot. I find that the more I include my boys in meal preparation, the more excited they are to try new things. Sometimes I will get some nice bread bowls from my grocery store, cut out the centers, and use them to serve the chili. Add your favorite toppings such as cheese, sour cream, and onions. Serve with a simple salad and Smoky Cheddar Skillet Cornbread (page 52).

Vegetable, Lime, and Chickpea Chili

2	tablespoons extra-virgin olive oil
1½	cups finely chopped white onion
1½	cups chopped zucchini
1½	cups chopped yellow squash
1	cup chopped mini sweet peppers
1	8-ounce package baby bella mushrooms, sliced
2	tablespoons minced garlic
2	15-ounce cans chickpeas, drained and rinsed
1	28-ounce can diced tomatoes
2	cups vegetable broth
½	cup chopped fresh cilantro leaves
3	tablespoons lime juice
2	teaspoons ground cumin
1	teaspoon chili powder
1	teaspoon kosher salt
½	teaspoon freshly ground black pepper
	Shredded cheddar cheese
	Sour cream
	Sliced green onions

1. Heat the olive oil in a Dutch oven or large pot over medium heat. Add the onion, zucchini, yellow squash, sweet peppers, and baby bellas and cook, stirring, until tender, 5 to 8 minutes. Add the garlic and cook, stirring, for 1 minute. Add the chickpeas, tomatoes, broth, cilantro, lime juice, cumin, chili powder, salt, and pepper, stir to combine, and cook until hot, about 5 minutes. Reduce the heat to low and simmer until ready to serve. Garnish with the cheddar cheese, sour cream, and green onions at the table.

Makes
6–8
Servings

Sliced fresh tomatoes, basil leaves, and mozzarella cheese baked over steamed white rice and drizzled with a balsamic dressing make for a simple side dish that serves well with many main dishes such as grilled chicken, beef, or fish. Steam your rice ahead of time to save time assembling. I like to have my boys help layer the cheese, basil, and tomatoes. This recipe also makes great leftovers.

Baked Rice Caprese

2	cups long-grain white rice
½	pound fresh mozzarella cheese, sliced ⅛ inch thick
8	to 10 large fresh basil leaves
4	medium vine-ripe tomatoes, sliced ⅛ inch thick
½	teaspoon kosher salt
¼	teaspoon freshly ground black pepper
¼	cup extra-virgin olive oil
2	tablespoons balsamic vinegar

1. Preheat the oven to 350°F and spray a 9×13-inch baking dish with nonstick cooking spray.

2. Bring a large saucepan with 2 cups of water to a boil. Stir in the rice, cover, and reduce the heat to low. Simmer for 20 minutes, until the water is absorbed. Transfer the cooked rice to the prepared baking dish.

3. Top the rice evenly with the mozzarella slices, basil leaves, and tomato slices and season with the salt and pepper. Add the olive oil and vinegar to a small bowl and whisk to combine. Drizzle over the top of the tomatoes. Bake for 30 to 35 minutes, until the cheese is melted.

Makes
8
Servings

It's so much fun playing around with different grilled cheese combinations. This particular mix of flavors is one of my favorites. I use a jar of roasted red peppers layered on top of mozzarella cheese sprinkled with one of my favorite spices, smoked paprika. Have the kids help layer on the cheese and roasted red peppers. These sandwiches are great for dipping in my 10-Minute Creamy Tomato Basil Soup (page 150).

Smoky Roasted Red Pepper and Mozzarella Grilled Cheese

8	slices bread (½ inch thick)
8	tablespoons (1 stick) butter, softened
8	slices fresh mozzarella (¼ inch thick)
1	cup chopped roasted red peppers
½	teaspoon smoked paprika

1. Heat a large skillet over medium heat and spray with nonstick cooking spray.

2. Spread 1 tablespoon of butter on one side of each slice of bread. In batches, place half the bread, butter side down, in the skillet. Layer with the cheese, roasted red peppers, and a pinch of smoked paprika. Place the remaining bread slices on top, butter side up, and cook until golden brown, 2 to 3 minutes per side. Remove from the skillet, cut in half, and serve warm.

Makes **4** Servings

Black beans make some of the best burgers. They are simple to prepare and quick to put together. This Mexican-style burger topped with my simple guacamole is a great way to enjoy a meatless meal without missing meat one bit. Have the kids help combine the burgers in the food processor; my boys love pressing the buttons. Serve with a simple salad and my Parmesan Roasted Carrot Fries (page 50).

Black Bean Guacamole Burgers

2	tablespoons extra-virgin olive oil
2	15-ounce cans black beans, drained and rinsed, divided
1	large egg
¼	cup chopped white onion
1	clove garlic
½	teaspoon kosher salt
¼	teaspoon freshly ground black pepper
¼	teaspoon garlic salt
1	cup Japanese panko bread crumbs
6	hamburger rolls, split
½	cup mayonnaise
6	large lettuce leaves
6	slices tomato (¼-inch thick)
	Party Guacamole (page 36)
	Tortilla chips

1. Heat the olive oil in a large skillet over medium heat.

2. Add half of the black beans, the egg, onion, garlic, salt, pepper, and garlic salt to a food processor. Pulse until well combined, and transfer to a medium mixing bowl. Add the bread crumbs and the remaining beans to the bowl and stir to combine. With your hands, form ½-cup each of the bean mixture into six patties.

3. In batches, add the patties to the hot skillet and cook until crispy, 3 to 4 minutes per side. In batches, add the rolls cut side down into the skillet to toast, 1 to 2 minutes. Remove and spread both sides of the rolls with the mayonnaise. Layer the bottoms of the rolls with 1 lettuce leaf, 1 bean burger, 1 tomato slice, and 2 to 3 tablespoons of guacamole. Close with the top of the roll. Serve with the remaining guacamole and a bowl of tortilla chips.

Makes
6
Servings

Pita bread is so versatile; we enjoy making personal-size pizzas on full pita rounds. Use my vegetable suggestions as just a guide and use whatever you have in the refrigerator or your family's favorites. Marinara sauce works as pizza sauce as well. The kids get a kick out of preparing their own pizza, so have them add their own toppings. Serve with a simple salad and my Homemade Ranch Dressing (page 202) for dipping if desired.

Veggie Pita Pizzas

4	whole pita breads
1	tablespoon extra-virgin olive oil
½	teaspoon garlic salt
1	cup pizza sauce
½	cup freshly grated Parmesan cheese
1	cup finely chopped mini sweet peppers
1	cup thinly sliced baby bella mushrooms
1	cup chopped baby spinach leaves
½	pound fresh mozzarella cheese, sliced ¼ inch thick

1. Preheat the oven to 400°F and spray a large baking sheet with nonstick cooking spray.

2. Place the pita breads on the prepared baking sheet. Brush with the olive oil, then season with the garlic salt. Spoon ¼ cup of the pizza sauce onto each pita, then top with 2 tablespoons of Parmesan cheese, ¼ cup sweet peppers, ¼ cup baby bellas, and ¼ cup spinach leaves. Top each with 3 slices mozzarella cheese. Bake for 12 to 15 minutes, until the cheese is melted. Let cool for 5 minutes, then cut into wedges.

Makes
4
Servings

Ever wanted to make your own red enchilada sauce, but afraid to try it? It's much easier than you think, with my simple recipe. Many store-bought sauces I buy seem to be too spicy for my kids, even the mild ones. You'll have leftover sauce that is great over burritos, Mexican casseroles, and even tacos. Simply place any remaining sauce in an airtight container and store in the freezer for another use. Enjoy this dish with my Spanish Rice (page 51) and Mini Bean and Cheese Burrito Cups (page 35).

Cheese Enchiladas with Homemade Sauce

2	tablespoons extra-virgin olive oil
2	cups finely chopped white onion
6	cloves garlic
1	28-ounce can crushed or diced tomatoes
1	cup reduced-sodium chicken broth
¼	cup cornmeal
¼	cup chili powder
2	tablespoons ground cumin
1	tablespoon packed light brown sugar
2	teaspoons smoked paprika
¾	teaspoon kosher salt
¼	teaspoon freshly ground black pepper
12	corn tortillas
4	cups shredded cheddar cheese, divided
2	cups shredded lettuce
1	cup diced tomatoes
½	cup sour cream

1. Preheat the oven to 350°F and spray a 9×13-inch baking dish with nonstick cooking spray.

2. Heat the olive oil in a Dutch oven or large pot over medium heat. Add the onion and garlic and cook, stirring, until tender, about 5 minutes. Add the tomatoes, chicken broth, cornmeal, chili powder, cumin, brown sugar, paprika, salt, and pepper and stir to combine. Reduce the heat to low and simmer for 15 minutes. In batches, transfer the sauce to a blender and blend until smooth. Return to the pot to simmer.

3. Pour 1 cup of the enchilada sauce into the bottom of the prepared baking dish. Warm the tortillas in a microwave oven for 60 seconds to make them easier to roll without tearing. Place ¼ cup of the cheddar cheese in the center of each tortilla, roll, and place seam side down in the baking dish. Repeat until all 12 tortillas have been filled and placed in the dish. Cover the tops of the tortillas with 1½ cups of the enchilada sauce, then top evenly with the remaining 1 cup cheddar cheese. (Freeze the remaining enchilada sauce for another use.) Bake for 25 to 30 minutes, until the cheese is melted. Serve with the shredded lettuce, diced tomatoes, and sour cream.

Makes **6** Servings

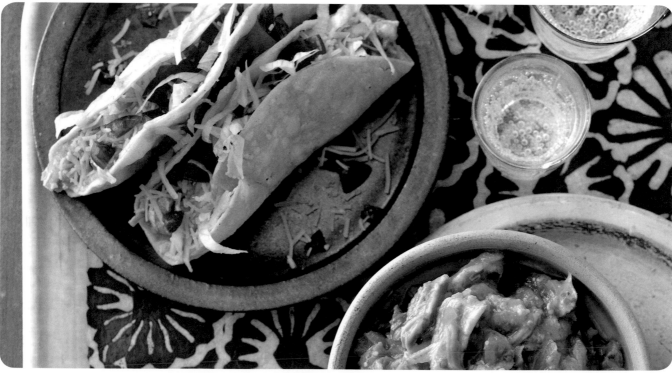

Slow and Low Recipes

Chapter 8

Recipes that take just minutes to prepare always score extra points with a busy cook. This soup has delicious enchilada flavors without all the work. Have the kids set the table while you prepare the soup, and by the time they are done, dinner is about ready. We love adding crushed tortilla chips and dollops of sour cream to our bowls. Serve with a simple green salad.

Chicken Enchilada Soup with Black Beans and Corn

2	tablespoons extra-virgin olive oil
1	cup finely chopped white onion
1	tablespoon minced garlic
3	cups shredded cooked chicken breast
1	15-ounce can black beans, drained and rinsed
1	15-ounce can sweet yellow corn, drained
1	10-ounce can tomatoes with green chilies, mild
1	10-ounce can red enchilada sauce, mild
2	cups reduced-sodium chicken broth
1	tablespoon fresh lime juice
1	teaspoon ground cumin
½	teaspoon kosher salt
¼	teaspoon freshly ground black pepper
2	cups crushed tortilla chips
1	cup sour cream

1. Heat the olive oil in a Dutch oven or large pot over medium heat. Add the onion and cook, stirring, until tender, about 5 minutes. Add the garlic and cook, stirring, for 1 minute. Add the chicken, black beans, corn, tomatoes, enchilada sauce, chicken broth, lime juice, cumin, salt, and pepper and stir to combine. Reduce the heat to low and simmer until ready to serve, at least 15 minutes.

2. To serve, place crushed tortilla chips in the bottoms of serving bowls, add the soup, and top with dollops of the sour cream.

Makes **6** Servings

Chicken and dumplings is one of those dinners that is pure comfort food. Chunky tender vegetables, shredded chicken, and tender dumplings make even the pickiest eaters ask for seconds. If you've never attempted dumplings, my recipe is a great one to start with. You add all of the ingredients in one bowl and use a cookie scoop to drop the dough right into the soup. This is a family favorite meal at our house that we make on a regular basis. Enjoy with a simple salad.

Chicken and Dumplings

2	tablespoons extra-virgin olive oil
1	cup peeled and diced carrot
1	cup finely chopped white onion
1	cup diced celery
2	tablespoons minced garlic
3½	cups reduced-sodium chicken broth
2½	cups shredded cooked chicken breast
2	tablespoons chopped fresh parsley
1½	teaspoons kosher salt, divided
½	teaspoon freshly ground black pepper
¾	cup cake flour
½	cup all-purpose flour
½	cup milk
¼	cup heavy cream
¼	cup cornmeal
1	teaspoon baking powder
¼	teaspoon smoked paprika

1. Heat the olive oil in a Dutch oven or large pot over medium heat. Add the carrot, onion, and celery and cook, stirring, until tender, 5 to 8 minutes. Add the garlic and cook, stirring, for 1 minute. Add the chicken broth, chicken, parsley, 1 teaspoon of the salt, and the pepper and cook, stirring, until hot, about 5 minutes.

2. To make the dumplings, add the flours, milk, heavy cream, cornmeal, baking powder, paprika, and the remaining ½ teaspoon salt to a large bowl. Stir until a sticky dough forms. With floured hands, knead for 30 seconds in the bowl. With a medium cookie scoop, drop the dough carefully into the pot, submerging the dumplings. Do not stir. Cover the pot, reduce to medium low, and cook until the dumplings are cooked through, about 10 minutes.

Makes
6
Servings

There is something really satisfying about cooking a nice pot of chili. As much as I love traditional red chili with tomatoes and chili powder, I also love a good white one with white beans and lots of cumin. Mine is full of vegetables and has a nice smoky flavor from the bacon. I love having my boys gather at the counter and help measure out all of the vegetables. Enjoy with my Smoky Cheddar Skillet Cornbread (page 52) or Cheesy Garlic Toast (page 31) and a simple green salad.

White Bean and Bacon Chicken Chili

½	pound bacon
1	Anaheim chile pepper
6	ounces pearl onions, peeled
1	cup peeled, shredded carrot
½	cup diced celery
1½	tablespoons minced garlic
32	ounces low-sodium chicken broth
2	cups shredded cooked chicken
2	15-ounce cans white beans, drained and rinsed
¼	cup chopped fresh cilantro
1	teaspoon ground cumin
½	teaspoon kosher salt
¼	teaspoon freshly ground black pepper

1. Separate the bacon into strips, add to a Dutch oven or large pot over medium heat, and cook, turning once or twice, until browned and crisp. Transfer the bacon to a paper towel–lined plate and discard all but 3 tablespoons of the drippings in pot. When bacon has cooled, crumble into small pieces. Cut the chile pepper in half lengthwise, remove the seeds and membrane, then dice the pepper. Heat the reserved bacon drippings over medium heat. Add the onions, carrot, celery, and chile pepper to the pot and cook, stirring, until tender, about 5 minutes. Add the garlic and cook, stirring, for 1 minute.

2. Add the chicken broth, chicken, crumbled bacon, beans, cilantro, cumin, salt, and pepper. Reduce the heat to low, and simmer for 15 minutes before serving.

Makes
6
Servings

I remember the day this recipe idea came to mind. I could hardly wait to prepare it, to see if it was as good as it was in my imagination. I wasn't sure how this soup would go over when I shared it on Picky Palate, but it continues to get rave reviews. It is so simple, takes only 15 minutes to prepare, and has all of the irresistible flavors of a BBQ chicken pizza. This soup works great as a light dinner or as a side to pizza and salad.

BBQ Chicken–Pizza Soup

2	tablespoons extra-virgin olive oil
1	cup finely chopped red onion
2	tablespoons minced garlic
2	cups shredded cooked chicken breast
1	11-ounce can corn with peppers, drained
1½	cups reduced-sodium chicken broth
1	cup chopped fresh cilantro leaves
½	cup prepared BBQ sauce
½	teaspoon kosher salt
¼	teaspoon freshly ground black pepper
¼	teaspoon garlic salt
1	cup shredded mozzarella cheese

1. Heat the olive oil in a Dutch oven or medium pot over medium heat. Add the onion and cook, stirring, until tender, about 5 minutes. Add the garlic and cook, stirring, for 1 minute. Add the chicken breast and corn and stir to combine. Add the chicken broth, cilantro, BBQ sauce, salt, pepper, and garlic salt and stir to combine. Reduce the heat to low and simmer for 5 to 10 minutes, until ready to serve. Garnish each bowl with shredded mozzarella cheese.

Makes
4–6
Servings

After one bite of a chicken and lime soup I ordered at a one of my family's favorite restaurants, I knew I had to go home and re-create all of the wonderful flavors I fell in love with. No kidding, I scurried home and developed this recipe that tastes nearly identical. This is now one of our favorite soups to prepare. Serve with dollops of avocado, shredded cheese, sour cream, and tortilla chips.

Green Chili Chicken and Lime Soup

2	tablespoons extra-virgin olive oil
1	cup finely chopped white onion
4	cloves garlic, minced
80	ounces reduced-sodium chicken broth
4	cups shredded cooked chicken breast
2½	cups cooked long-grain white rice
1	10-ounce can tomatoes with green chilies, mild
1	7-ounce can diced green chilies
¼	cup fresh lime juice, plus more for drizzling over avocados
1½	teaspoons ground cumin
½	teaspoon kosher salt
¼	teaspoon freshly ground black pepper
¼	teaspoon garlic salt
1½	cups chopped fresh cilantro leaves
2	avocados, peeled, seeded, diced, and drizzled with lime juice
1	cup shredded cheddar cheese
1	cup sour cream
2	cups crushed tortilla chips

1. Heat the olive oil in a Dutch oven or large pot over medium heat. Add the onion and cook, stirring, until tender, about 5 minutes. Add the garlic and cook, stirring, for 1 minute. Add the chicken broth, chicken, rice, tomatoes, green chilies, lime juice, cumin, salt, pepper, and garlic salt and cook, stirring, for 5 minutes. Reduce the heat to low. Add the cilantro and stir to combine.

2. Serve with the avocado, cheddar cheese, sour cream, and crushed tortilla chips.

Makes
10–12
Servings

I shared this recipe on *Picky Palate* a couple years ago, and it has been a reader favorite ever since. It's chock-full of vegetables, chicken, and healthy quinoa. Quinoa has the taste and texture of a cross between brown rice and oatmeal. It is also high in protein and can be found in most health food stores. I love taking my ingredient list to the store with the boys and having them pick out the vegetables needed to make dinner. Enjoy with my Smoky Cheddar Skillet Cornbread (page 52) or Cheesy Garlic Toast (page 31).

Healthy and Hearty Chicken Quinoa Stew

1	cup quinoa
2	tablespoons extra-virgin olive oil
4	cups shredded cooked chicken breasts
¾	teaspoon kosher salt, divided
½	teaspoon freshly ground black pepper, divided
1½	cups finely chopped white onion
1	cup finely chopped celery
4	large carrots, peeled and sliced
2	cups mini sweet peppers, chopped
1½	cups chopped zucchini
64	ounces chicken broth
1	15-ounce can diced tomatoes
5	medium Yukon gold potatoes, scrubbed and cubed into 1-inch pieces
1½	cups fresh parsley, chopped
2	tablespoons Dijon mustard
1	tablespoon hot sauce, like Tabasco
¼	teaspoon garlic salt

1. Rinse the quinoa in warm water. Bring 2 cups of water to a boil in 2-quart saucepan. Add the quinoa, bring back to a boil, cover, and cook over medium heat for 12 minutes, until water is absorbed. Remove from heat, fluff, and let stand for 15 minutes.

2. Heat the olive oil in a Dutch oven or large pot over medium heat. Season the chicken with ¼ teaspoon of the salt and ¼ teaspoon of the pepper. Toss gently and set aside. Add the onion, celery, carrots, sweet peppers, and zucchini and cook, stirring, until softened, 10 to 15 minutes. Add the chicken broth, tomatoes, and potatoes, stirring to combine, and increase to high heat just until broth starts to boil. Reduce the heat back to medium high and cook until the potatoes are fork tender, about 10 minutes. Reduce the heat to low and add the parsley, Dijon mustard, hot sauce, garlic salt, cooked quinoa, chicken, and the remaining ½ teaspoon salt and ¼ teaspoon pepper. Stir to combine, and simmer until ready to serve.

Makes
8–10
Servings

This Southwest chicken chili has been made countless times in our home. I often use this recipe when one of my friends or neighbors is in need of a meal. It's warm without being spicy and goes perfectly with my Smoky Cheddar Skillet Cornbread (page 52) or Cheesy Garlic Toast (page 31). Often I pick up a prepared rotisserie chicken from the grocery store when I need a shortcut from baking my own chicken. Enjoy with a simple salad and your favorite chili toppings.

Southwest Shredded Chicken 3-Bean Chili

2	tablespoons extra-virgin olive oil
1¼	cups finely chopped white onion
1	cup diced green bell pepper
4	cloves minced garlic
42	ounces reduced-sodium chicken broth
4	cups shredded cooked chicken
1	15-ounce can black beans, drained and rinsed
1	15-ounce can red kidney beans, drained and rinsed
1	15-ounce can cannellini beans, drained and rinsed
1	15-ounce can fire-roasted diced tomatoes
6	ounces tomato paste
2	tablespoons chili powder
1	tablespoon hot sauce, like Tabasco
1	tablespoon fresh lime juice
1	tablespoon ground cumin
1¼	teaspoons kosher salt
½	teaspoon freshly ground black pepper
1	cup sour cream
1	cup shredded cheddar cheese
1	cup chopped green onions

1. Heat the olive oil in a Dutch oven or large pot over medium heat. Add the onion and bell pepper and cook, stirring, until tender, about 5 minutes. Add the garlic and cook, stirring, for 1 minute. Add the chicken broth, chicken, all the beans, the tomatoes, tomato paste, chili powder, hot sauce, lime juice, cumin, salt, and pepper and cook, stirring, for 5 minutes. Reduce the heat to low and simmer until ready to serve. Top the bowls with dollops of sour cream, the cheddar cheese, and green onions.

Makes 8–10 Servings

Chicken noodle soup makes everything better, doesn't it? It's guaranteed to brighten your day, especially if you are under the weather. This hearty recipe is full of tender vegetables, noodles, and shredded chicken nestled in a delightfully seasoned broth. I prefer using broken pieces of spaghetti noodles; however, any small noodles will work just fine. This soup is great for packaging up in mason jars to give to family and friends or for enjoying on chilly days. Treat yourself with my Smoky Cheddar Skillet Cornbread (page 52) for dipping, and enjoy with a simple salad.

Warm Home-Style Chicken Noodle Soup

2	tablespoons extra-virgin olive oil
4	cups chopped fresh spinach leaves
2	cups peeled and diced carrot
1½	cups diced celery
1¼	cups finely chopped white onion
2	cloves garlic, minced
64	ounces reduced-sodium chicken broth
4	cups shredded cooked chicken
¼	pound thin spaghetti
1	tablespoon whole-grain Dijon mustard
¾	teaspoon kosher salt
¼	teaspoon freshly ground black pepper
¼	teaspoon garlic salt

1. Heat the olive oil in a Dutch oven or large pot over medium heat. Add the spinach, carrot, celery, and onion and cook, stirring, until tender, about 8 minutes. Add the garlic and cook, stirring, for 1 minute. Add the chicken broth and chicken and stir to combine. Increase the heat to high until just starting to boil. Break the spaghetti into 1-inch pieces, add to the pot, stir, reduce the heat to low, and cook until the noodles are tender, about 7 minutes. Add the mustard, salt, pepper, and garlic salt and stir to combine. Simmer until ready to serve.

Makes
6–8
Servings

I am a huge fan of soup with some substance. I like chunky soup with interesting layers of flavor. This soup is just that—it's full of texture and complexity that make it a family favorite. Fresh corn is ideal in this recipe, but frozen works too. Serve this recipe as a main dish, with a simple salad and crusty bread, or serve as a side to go with your favorite chicken, beef, or seafood entrée.

Hearty Ham and Cheddar Corn Chowder

3	tablespoons extra-virgin olive oil
1½	cups finely chopped white onion
1½	cups peeled and diced carrot
1	cup chopped celery
2	cloves garlic, minced
½	pound ham, cut into a ½-inch dice
2	pounds fresh or frozen corn kernels
3	14-ounce cans reduced-sodium chicken broth
8	ounces sour cream
1	cup half-and-half
1	cup shredded cheddar cheese
½	teaspoon kosher salt
¼	teaspoon freshly ground black pepper
¼	teaspoon garlic salt

1. Heat the olive oil in a Dutch oven or large pot over medium heat. Add the onion, carrot, and celery and cook, stirring, until tender, 10 to 12 minutes. Add the garlic and cook, stirring, for 1 minute. Add the ham and cook, stirring, until hot, about 3 minutes.

2. Add half of the corn to a food processor and pulse until nearly smooth. Pour the mixture into the pot and add the remaining whole kernels. Add the chicken broth, sour cream, and half-and-half and cook, stirring, until hot, about 5 minutes. Add the cheese and stir until melted. Reduce the heat to low and season with the salt, pepper, and garlic salt. Serve hot.

Makes 6–8 Servings

A soup that can be made in about 10 minutes is priceless when you've got a house full of hungry mouths to feed. Cans of diced tomatoes are so versatile. I make sure that I have at least a few cans on hand every week for simple dinner ideas including this simple soup. The boys love being in charge of pressing the buttons of the blender or food processor, so they love helping with this recipe. Grilled cheese and tomato soup go hand in hand. Try my Smoky Roasted Red Pepper and Mozzarella Grilled Cheese (page 133) for dipping, along with a simple salad.

10-Minute Creamy Tomato-Basil Soup

2	15-ounce cans diced tomatoes
¼	cup finely chopped white onion
2	cloves garlic, minced
12	fresh basil leaves
1	teaspoon kosher salt
½	teaspoon freshly ground black pepper
½	cup heavy cream

1. Add the tomatoes, onion, garlic, basil, salt, and pepper to a food processor or blender. Pulse or blend until smooth.

2. Pour the soup into a medium saucepan set over medium-low heat. Add the heavy cream, stir to combine, and cook for 5 minutes, stirring, until hot. Serve warm.

Makes
4
Servings

Nothing spells comfort food better than a piping hot bowl of hearty soup. You'll find that this soup is packed with a beautiful variety of vegetables in a nicely seasoned broth that the entire family enjoys. I like to round up the boys to help add all the colorful vegetables to the pot. Get the kids involved—they'll love having a hand in this recipe. Break out your extra-large pot. This recipe makes enough to feed your neighbors and friends. Add a nice spoonful of freshly grated Parmesan cheese right before serving, along with buttered toast or rolls for dipping.

Hearty Minestrone

3	tablespoons extra-virgin olive oil
1½	cups diced ham
2	cups finely chopped white onion
2	cups thinly sliced baby bella mushrooms
2	cups peeled and diced carrot
2	cups chopped zucchini
1	cup chopped yellow squash
1	cup diced celery
32	ounces reduced-sodium chicken broth
2	15-ounce cans white beans, drained and rinsed
1	10-ounce can diced tomatoes
½	cup freshly grated Parmesan cheese
1	tablespoon brown mustard
1¾	teaspoons kosher salt
½	teaspoon freshly ground black pepper
½	teaspoon garlic salt
½	teaspoon dried basil

1. Heat the olive oil in a Dutch oven or large pot over medium heat. Add the ham and cook, stirring, until hot, about 5 minutes. Add the onion, baby bellas, carrot, zucchini, squash, and celery and cook, stirring, until tender, about 10 minutes.

2. Add the chicken broth, white beans, tomatoes, Parmesan cheese, mustard, salt, pepper, garlic salt, and basil and cook, stirring, until hot, about 5 minutes. Reduce the heat to low and simmer until ready to serve.

Makes
8–10
Servings

Memories of living with my grandparents vividly come to mind when I think of warm beef stew. My sweet Granna would often prepare a delicious beef stew similar to the one I have developed for my family. Make sure to pick up your favorite soft rolls from the grocery store to serve with this dish along with a simple salad.

Good Old-Fashioned Slow-Cooker Beef Stew

1	cup all-purpose flour
1½	teaspoons kosher salt, divided
1	teaspoon freshly ground black pepper, divided
1	pound beef stew meat
¼	cup extra-virgin olive oil, divided
3	stalks celery, cut into ½-inch pieces
3	carrots, peeled and cut into ½-inch pieces
6	ounces sliced white mushrooms
1½	cups pearl onions, peeled
4	medium potatoes, cut into ½-inch chunks
3	cloves garlic, minced
32	ounces beef broth
1	tablespoon Worcestershire sauce

1. Heat a slow cooker on the high setting. Add the flour, 1 teaspoon of the salt, and ½ teaspoon of the pepper to a large zip-top bag and shake the bag to combine. Add the stew meat, shaking the bag to coat, then remove the beef, shaking off excess flour.

2. Heat 2 tablespoons of the olive oil in a Dutch oven or large pot over medium heat. Add the floured beef to the pot and brown on both sides, turning once, about 5 minutes per side. Add the remaining 2 tablespoons olive oil to the pot and add the celery, carrots, mushrooms, onions, potatoes, and garlic. Cook, stirring, until the vegetables are tender, about 10 minutes. Transfer the beef and vegetables to the slow cooker. Add the beef broth, Worcestershire sauce, and the remaining ½ teaspoon salt and ½ teaspoon pepper and stir to combine. Cover with the lid and cook until the beef is fork tender, on low for 6 to 8 hours or on high for 4 to 5 hours.

Makes
6
Servings

These simple slow-cooked pork tacos are a reader favorite recipe on Picky Palate. These are some of the most flavorful pulled pork tacos I've ever eaten. With just a few ingredients, you'll have everything in the slow cooker in about 5 minutes. We like to enjoy these on soft tortilla bread or naan bread; however, soft or crunchy taco shells are delicious too. I like to have my boys help measure all of the vegetables and help set the table. Top with your favorite taco toppings.

Slow-Cooked Green Chili Pork Tacos

1	3- to 4-pound pork butt
2	tablespoons Worcestershire sauce
1	tablespoon kosher salt
1	teaspoon freshly ground black pepper
½	teaspoon garlic salt
2	cups mild tomatillo salsa
10	to 15 tortillas of choice
2	cups shredded lettuce
2	cups diced tomatoes
2	cups shredded cheese
1	cup sour cream

1. Heat a slow cooker to the high setting.

2. Add ½ cup of water to the slow cooker. Add the pork butt and season with the Worcestershire sauce, salt, pepper, and garlic salt. Cover and cook on high for 5 to 7 hours. Remove the pork from the jus (discard or reserve for another use). Shred the pork into small, bite-size pieces, return to the slow cooker, and add the salsa. Reduce the slow cooker heat to low until ready to serve. Serve the pork in soft tortilla bread or regular corn tortillas along with the lettuce, tomatoes, cheese, and sour cream.

Makes
10–15
Servings

This recipe has Sunday dinner written all over it. There's something beautiful about a hearty, slow-cooked meal with delicious leftovers to enjoy the next day. Try preparing this meal in the morning so you can enjoy the aroma all day long; it's quite rewarding. After hours of slow cooking, you'll have the most tender short ribs in a vegetable-packed broth that demands thick slices of buttered bread for dipping.

Braised Short Ribs and Vegetables

½	cup extra-virgin olive oil, divided
5	stalks celery, cut into 1-inch pieces
3	large carrots, cut into 1-inch pieces
1	large white onion, peeled and quartered
2	large russet potatoes, peeled and diced into 1-inch pieces
5	cloves garlic
¾	cup all-purpose flour
1	teaspoon kosher salt
½	teaspoon freshly ground black pepper
½	teaspoon garlic salt
1½	to 2 pounds boneless short ribs
2	cups beef broth
3	tablespoons Worcestershire sauce

1. Heat a slow cooker on the high setting and add 4 tablespoons of the olive oil. Add the celery, carrots, onion, potatoes, and garlic and cook, stirring to combine, then cover.

2. Add the flour, salt, pepper, and garlic salt to a large zip-top bag and shake the bag to combine. Add the short ribs one at a time, coating all sides with the flour.

3. Heat the remaining 4 tablespoons of the oil in a Dutch oven or large pot over medium heat. Add the floured short ribs and cook until browned, about 6 minutes each side. Transfer the browned short ribs to the slow cooker and nestle into vegetables. Add the beef broth and Worcestershire sauce, cover, and cook on high for 4 to 5 hours.

Makes **6–8** Servings

If your home is anything like ours, taco night happens regularly. I love preparing this recipe in the morning and letting it simmer all day in the slow cooker while enjoying the aromas that fill the air. Cooking taco meat in the slow cooker really gives a nice slow-cooked restaurant quality taste to your tacos. If you are short of time, this recipe is great prepared on the stovetop as well. Top your tacos with shredded lettuce, cheese, sour cream, and Teedo's Famous Salsa (page 33). Serve with my Spanish Rice (page 51).

Slow-Cooker Ground Beef Tacos

2	tablespoons extra-virgin olive oil
1	cup finely chopped white onion
¼	cup chopped mini sweet peppers
3	cloves garlic, minced
1	pound lean ground beef
½	teaspoon kosher salt
¼	teaspoon freshly ground black pepper
1	10-ounce can diced tomatoes with green chilies
½	cup prepared mild salsa
2	tablespoons fresh lime juice
1	teaspoon ground cumin
¼	cup chopped fresh cilantro
8	to 10 tortillas of choice
2	cups shredded lettuce
1	cup shredded cheddar cheese
1	cup sour cream

1. Heat a slow cooker on the low setting.

2. Heat the olive oil in a Dutch oven or large pot over medium heat. Add the onion and sweet peppers and cook, stirring, until tender, about 5 minutes. Add the garlic and cook, stirring, for 1 minute. Add the ground beef, salt, and pepper and cook, stirring and breaking up the meat until browned. Drain the fat from the pan if necessary. Transfer the mixture to the slow cooker and add the tomatoes, salsa, lime juice, cumin, and cilantro and stir to combine. Simmer on low until ready to serve, at least 2 hours. Serve in tortillas and top with the lettuce, cheese, and sour cream.

Makes
{8–10}
Servings

Breaking out the slow cooker makes me so happy. I love preparing slow-cooker meals either the night before I plan on serving them or the morning of. There is something special about coming home for the day or waking up in the morning to smells of your slow-cooked meal filling the air. Have the kids help measure all of the vegetables to add to the pot. Add a big spoonful of freshly grated Parmesan cheese to each bowl before serving along with thick crusty bread for dipping.

Slow-Cooked Italian Beef and Pesto Stew

½	cup all-purpose flour
1½	teaspoons kosher salt, divided
¾	teaspoon freshly ground black pepper, divided
1	pound beef stew meat
¼	cup extra-virgin olive oil, divided
2	cups sliced carrot
1	cup diced celery
1½	cups finely chopped white onion
4	cloves garlic
32	ounces beef broth
1	14.5-ounce can petite diced tomatoes
3	tablespoons prepared pesto
½	teaspoon dried oregano
½	cup freshly grated Parmesan cheese

1. Heat a slow cooker on the high setting.

2. Add the flour, 1 teaspoon of the salt, and ½ teaspoon of the pepper to a large zip-top plastic bag and shake the bag to combine. Add the stew meat and shake the bag to coat the beef.

3. Heat 2 tablespoons of the olive oil in a Dutch oven or large pot over medium heat. Shake the excess flour from the stew meat, then add to the pot. Cook until a nice brown crust forms on each side, 3 to 5 minutes per side. Add the remaining 2 tablespoons of olive oil to the pot. Add the carrot, celery, and onion and cook, stirring, until tender, about 10 minutes. Add the garlic and cook, stirring, for 1 minute.

4. Add the beef broth, tomatoes, pesto, and oregano, and the remaining ½ teaspoon salt and ¼ teaspoon pepper and stir to combine. Transfer the stew to the slow cooker and cook on high for 5 hours. Top each bowl with a spoonful of Parmesan cheese.

Makes 10–12 Servings

Such great memories come to mind when I think of pot roast dinner. I'm quickly taken back to Sundays with our family in Arizona where the kids are running around, wrestling with each other, and asking if dinner is done yet. The aroma of the roast and vegetables fills the whole house, which leads to sneaking bites while no one is looking. My slow-cooked pot roast is tender, juicy, full of flavor, and takes just minutes to get in the slow cooker. Make sure you save your leftover strained jus from the slow cooker for the Pot Roast French Dip Sandwiches (page 96).

Classic Slow-Cooked Pot Roast and Vegetables

1	4- to 5-pound boneless beef chuck pot roast
1½	teaspoons kosher salt
½	teaspoon freshly ground black pepper
½	teaspoon garlic salt
3	cups unpeeled diced potatoes (1-inch pieces)
2	cups peeled baby carrots
6	stalks celery, cut into 1-inch pieces
10	ounces white pearl onions, peeled
½	cup Worcestershire sauce
5	cloves garlic

1. Heat a slow cooker on the high setting.

2. Season both sides of the roast with the salt, pepper, and garlic salt and add to the slow cooker. Add the potatoes, carrots, celery, onions, 1 cup of water, the Worcestershire sauce, and garlic. Cover and cook on high for 5 hours or low for 8 to 10 hours.

3. Remove the roast from the slow cooker and break into individual servings. Serve with the vegetables. Strain the liquid and save to make au jus sandwiches with any leftover roast.

Makes
8–10
Servings

Chapter 9

Sweet Tooth

Cakes, Pies, and More

Does it get much better than warm homemade apple pie with vanilla ice cream dripping down the sides? Bookmark this recipe when you've got extra time to play in the kitchen. It takes a little time to prepare, but when it comes out of the oven golden brown with that sweet cinnamon-apple aroma filling the house, it's all worth it. My pie crust is simple to prepare and is buttery and flaky, just how it should be. Have the kids help roll out the crust and lay it inside the pie plate over the apples. Serve each slice of pie warm with a scoop of your favorite vanilla ice cream on top.

Homemade Apple Pie

For the crust

2¾	cups all-purpose flour
4	tablespoons granulated sugar, divided
1	teaspoon kosher salt
8	ounces (2 sticks) cold unsalted butter, cubed
½	cup ice water
1	large egg white

For the filling

3	pounds Granny Smith apples, thinly sliced (about 10 cups)
2	tablespoons fresh lemon juice
½	cup granulated sugar
¼	cup all-purpose flour
½	teaspoon kosher salt

1. To make the crust, add the flour, 3 tablespoons of the sugar, and the salt to a food processor. Pulse to combine. Add the butter and pulse until the mixture is the size of small peas. With the processor running, slowly add the ice water until combined. Transfer the dough to a lightly floured countertop, kneading a couple of times to combine. Divide the dough in half, flatten slightly, and wrap tightly with plastic wrap. Refrigerate for 2 to 3 hours.

2. Preheat the oven to 350°F and spray a deep 9-inch pie plate with nonstick cooking spray.

3. To make the filling, add the sliced apples to a large bowl and drizzle with the lemon juice, tossing to combine. Add the sugar, flour, and salt and stir to combine.

4. Remove the pie dough from the plastic wrap and place onto a lightly floured countertop. Roll each piece of dough to a 10-inch round. Place one rolled crust into the bottom of the prepared pie plate, pressing gently around the bottom and up the sides of the plate. Pour the apple filling into the pie plate. Place the second rolled pie crust over the apple filling and crimp the edges as desired to enclose the filling.

5. With a knife, cut 3 to 5 slits in the crust's top to allow steam to escape. Whisk the egg white with 1 teaspoon of water, brush over the top of the pie, then sprinkle with the remaining 1 tablespoon sugar. Bake for 65 to 80 minutes, until the crust is golden and the filling is bubbling. Let cool for 30 minutes before cutting into slices.

Makes 8–10 Servings

Dare I say that warm bread pudding might be the most tempting dessert ever? There's something about digging my spoon into warm, sweet, cinnamon-scented, custard-like pudding that makes me giddy. As if this dessert weren't decadent enough, I've topped it off with a buttery caramel sauce for your enjoyment. Have the kids help by topping with ice cream or whipped cream.

Cinnamon Swirl Bread Pudding with Caramel Sauce

5	cups ½-inch-cubed sweet Hawaiian bread
1½	cups granulated sugar
5	large eggs
1	cup whole milk
1	cup heavy cream
2	tablespoons ground cinnamon
2	teaspoons vanilla extract
½	cup packed light brown sugar
1	tablespoon water
2	tablespoons unsalted butter
3	tablespoons sour cream

1. Preheat the oven to 350°F and spray a 9×13-inch baking dish with nonstick cooking spray.

2. Spread the bread cubes in the bottom of the prepared baking dish. Add the sugar, eggs, milk, heavy cream, cinnamon, and vanilla to a large bowl and whisk until well combined. Pour the egg mixture over the bread cubes and bake 35 to 40 minutes, until set. Remove from oven.

3. To make the caramel sauce, add the brown sugar and the water to a small saucepan over medium heat and stir to combine. Let bubble and boil for 5 minutes, then add the butter and sour cream, stirring until smooth. Drizzle the caramel sauce over the warm bread pudding and serve.

Makes **8** Servings

There is nothing my husband loves more than yellow cake with chocolate frosting for his birthday. After years of taking the easy way out and using cake mixes, I spent months creating the perfect yellow butter cake. It is buttery sweet and moist, just how we like it. For another variation, once the cakes are cooled, spread ¾ cup of your favorite jam over the first layer, place the top layer over the jam, and frost the top and sides with my Cream Cheese Frosting (page 203).

Homemade Yellow Butter Cake with Chocolate Cream Frosting

8	ounces (2 sticks) unsalted butter, softened
2¼	cups granulated sugar
4	large eggs
¼	cup sour cream
1	tablespoon vanilla extract
¼	cup milk
¼	cup buttermilk
3	cups cake flour
1	tablespoon baking powder
1½	teaspoons kosher salt

Chocolate-Buttercream Frosting

12	ounces cream cheese, softened
12	tablespoons (1½ sticks) unsalted butter, softened
1½	cups semi-sweet chocolate chips
5¼	cups powdered sugar
¼	cup plus 2 tablespoons cocoa powder

1. Preheat the oven to 350°F and generously spray two 9-inch cake pans with nonstick cooking spray.

2. Add the butter and sugar to the bowl of a stand mixer and beat until light and fluffy. Add the eggs, sour cream, and vanilla, beating until well combined. Add the milk and buttermilk to a small bowl and stir to combine. Set aside.

3. Add the flour, baking powder, and salt to a large bowl and stir to combine. With the mixer on low, first add half of the dry ingredients, then add half of the milk mixture, then add the remaining dry ingredients, and end with the remaining milk mixture, beating until well combined, about 1 minute.

4. Divide the batter between the prepared cake pans, spreading evenly. Bake for 35 to 40 minutes, until a toothpick comes out clean from the center of the cakes. Let cool for 30 minutes before removing the cakes from the pans and let cool completely before frosting.

5. To make the frosting, add the cream cheese and butter to the bowl of a stand mixer and beat until well combined. In a microwave-safe bowl, melt the chocolate in the microwave in 30-second intervals, stirring until smooth. Slowly add the melted chocolate to the mixer bowl, beating until well combined. Slowly add the powdered sugar and cocoa powder, mixing until well combined.

6. Place one of the cooled cakes onto a cake stand. Spread some of the frosting over the top of the cake, then place the second cake on top. Add the remaining frosting to the top and spread over the top and sides of the cake. Serve the cake at room temperature or chill until ready to serve.

Makes 10–12 Servings

I have been perfecting homemade chocolate cupcake recipes for years, and I am happy to say I have created what we think is the perfect recipe. You can also use this recipe for a layered chocolate cake that is great for birthdays and other celebrations. Divide the batter between two 9-inch cake pans and bake for 25 to 30 minutes, until cooked through. The kids love to be in charge of the mixer for this recipe. You can also use Chocolate Buttercream Frosting for your cupcakes (page 203).

Soft Double-Chocolate Cupcakes with Cream Cheese Frosting

1	cup semi-sweet chocolate chips
½	cup milk
¾	cup all-purpose flour
⅓	cup cocoa powder
1	cup granulated sugar
½	teaspoon kosher salt
½	teaspoon baking soda
2	large eggs
½	cup sour cream
½	cup canola oil
2	teaspoons vanilla extract

Cream Cheese Frosting

1	8-ounce package cream cheese, softened
8	tablespoons (1 stick) unsalted butter, softened
3	cups powdered sugar

1. Preheat the oven to 350°F and line two 12-count muffin pans with 19 cupcake liners.

2. Finely chop the chocolate chips and place in a medium-size bowl. In a microwave-safe cup, heat the milk in the microwave until hot, 60 to 90 seconds. Pour the hot milk over the chopped chocolate chips. Let sit for 2 minutes, then stir until smooth and melted.

3. Add the flour, cocoa powder, sugar, salt, and baking soda to a large bowl and mix to combine. Add the eggs, sour cream, canola oil, and vanilla to a stand mixer and mix on medium speed until well combined, about 1 minute. Slowly add the melted chocolate, followed by the dry ingredients, mixing until combined, about 1 minute. Fill the cupcake liners half full and bake for 15 to 17 minutes, until a toothpick comes out clean from the center of the cupcakes. Let cool completely.

4. To make the cream cheese frosting, add the cream cheese and butter to the bowl of a stand mixer and beat on medium speed until smooth. Slowly add the powdered sugar, beating until well combined. Spread the frosting on the cooled cupcakes.

Makes
19
Cupcakes

In 2008, I was on Food Network's Ultimate Recipe Showdown and competed with a roasted banana bread drop doughnut recipe. The judges enjoyed my recipe, but alas, it did not take the grand prize. I re-created my doughnuts into a chocolate version that I like even better than the original. The thick, sweet glaze pushes them over the top. My boys love to help glaze each little doughnut and watch carefully as they set up. Serve warm, at room temperature, or chilled with a tall glass of milk.

Sweet Glazed Chocolate Banana Bread Doughnut Holes

4	cups vegetable or canola oil
1¾	cups all-purpose flour
½	cup granulated sugar
½	cup cocoa powder
1	teaspoon baking powder
½	teaspoon baking soda
½	teaspoon kosher salt
¼	cup heavy cream
¼	cup milk
¼	cup sour cream
1	large egg
3	ripe bananas, mashed
2	cups powdered sugar
¾	to 1 cup heavy cream

1. Heat the oil in a Dutch oven or large pot over medium heat to 350°F on a thermometer.

2. Add the flour, granulated sugar, cocoa powder, baking powder, baking soda, and salt to a large bowl and stir to combine.

3. Add the cream, milk, sour cream, and egg to a small bowl and whisk to combine. Add the wet ingredients to the dry ingredients, then add the mashed bananas, stirring, until just combined.

4. With a small cookie scoop, scoop the dough, carefully drop into the hot oil, and fry until crisped on the outside and cooked through, 3 to 4 minutes. Transfer the doughnuts to a paper towel–lined plate to drain.

5. Add the powdered sugar and cream to a medium bowl and whisk until smooth and a good drizzling consistency. Drizzle the glaze over both sides of the doughnuts. Serve warm or at room temperature.

Makes 18–22 Donuts

There is something so special about a homemade pie sitting on the counter to be enjoyed, especially a vibrant blueberry pie. My simple recipe will have you impressing your family and friends in no time. I love having my boys help roll out the pie crust and press it into the pie plate. They also love stirring the blueberry filling and pouring it into the pie crust. Enjoy this pie warm with a nice scoop of vanilla ice cream.

Homemade Blueberry Pie

For the crust

2¾	cups all-purpose flour
4	tablespoons granulated sugar, divided
1	teaspoon kosher salt
8	ounces (2 sticks) cold unsalted butter, cubed
½	cup ice water
1	large egg white

For the filling

4	cups fresh or frozen blueberries
¾	cup granulated sugar
3	tablespoons cornstarch
1	tablespoon fresh lemon juice

1. To make the crust, add the flour, 3 tablespoons of the sugar, and the salt to a food processor. Pulse to combine. Add the butter and pulse until the mixture is the size of small peas. With the processor running, slowly add the ice water until combined. Transfer the dough to a lightly floured countertop, kneading a couple of times to combine. Divide the dough in half, flatten slightly, and wrap tightly with plastic wrap. Refrigerate for 2 to 3 hours.

2. Preheat the oven to 350°F and spray a deep 9-inch pie plate with nonstick cooking spray.

3. To make the filling, add the blueberries, sugar, and cornstarch to a large bowl, tossing to combine. Add the lemon juice and toss to combine. Remove the pie dough from the plastic wrap and place onto a lightly floured countertop. Roll each piece of dough into a 10-inch round. Place one rolled crust into the bottom of the prepared pie plate, pressing gently around the bottom and up the sides of the plate. Pour the blueberry filling into the pie plate. Place the second rolled pie crust over the blueberry filling and crimp the edges as desired to enclose the filling.

4. With a knife, cut 3 to 5 slits in the crust's top to allow steam to escape. Whisk the egg white with 1 teaspoon of water, brush over the top of the pie, then sprinkle with the remaining 1 tablespoon sugar. Bake for 65 to 80 minutes, until the crust is golden and the filling is bubbling. Let cool for 30 minutes before cutting into slices.

Makes 8–10 Servings

This simple rustic pie is a great dessert for your family and friends. The vibrant purple pie filling bubbles through the crust as it bakes and sends you racing for the vanilla ice cream and a spoon. Serve hot, topped with ice cream, so it melts into a soupy treat at the bottom of your bowl. I love watching the look on my boys' faces when they take their first bite of this one—pure enjoyment. You can also make a delicious Homemade Pie Crust (page 203).

Rustic Blueberry-Raspberry Pie

2 cups fresh or frozen blueberries

2 cups fresh or frozen raspberries

¾ cup plus 1 tablespoon granulated sugar

3 tablespoons cornstarch

1 tablespoon fresh lemon juice

1 9-inch refrigerated pie crust, at room temperature

1 large egg white

1 pint vanilla ice cream

1. Preheat the oven to 350°F and spray a 9-inch cast-iron skillet with nonstick cooking spray.

2. Add the blueberries, raspberries, ¾ cup of the sugar, and the cornstarch to a large bowl and toss to combine. Add the lemon juice and toss to combine. Pour into the prepared cast-iron skillet. Lay the pie crust over the top, gently pressing the edges around the pan. Cut 3 to 5 slits in the crust to allow steam to escape.

3. Add the egg white and 1 teaspoon of water to a small bowl and whisk to combine. Brush a light layer of the egg wash over the pie, then sprinkle the remaining 1 tablespoon sugar over the top. Bake 45 to 55 minutes, until crust is cooked through and golden brown. Serve warm with scoops of vanilla ice cream.

Makes
4
Servings

I used to pay big bucks for soft salted caramels at specialty candy shops before I decided to perfect my own recipe. You'll need a candy thermometer, which you can find at most grocery stores or any kitchen store. I adore my little jar of fleur de sel sea salt. Fleur de sel is known as the aroma of violets that develops as the salt is drying in France. You can substitute kosher salt if needed. These caramels are great cut into squares or wrapped in parchment paper for gifts any time of the year. Round up the family and have everyone help wrap the caramels in parchment paper.

Homemade Salted Soft Caramels

5	tablespoons unsalted butter
1	cup heavy cream
1	teaspoon vanilla extract
1¾	cups granulated sugar
1½	teaspoons fleur de sel sea salt or kosher salt, divided

1. Line an 8×8-inch baking pan with parchment paper and spray lightly with nonstick cooking spray.

2. Add the butter, cream, and vanilla to a small saucepan over medium heat, stirring to melt, then bring to a low boil. Once the mixture starts to boil, remove from the heat and set aside.

3. Add the sugar, ½ cup of water, and 1 teaspoon of the salt to a large saucepan over medium heat, stirring to dissolve, then bring to a boil. Let the syrup boil without stirring, only occasionally swirling the pan, until it is a deep golden brown, 6 to 8 minutes. Reduce the heat to low, and slowly add the cream mixture while stirring constantly. The mixture will bubble violently, but keep stirring. Place a candy thermometer into the saucepan, touching the caramel but not touching the bottom of the pan. Cook, stirring, until the temperature reaches 248°F (firm ball stage on a candy thermometer). Remove immediately and pour into the prepared baking pan. Sprinkle with the remaining ½ teaspoon salt and let cool for 30 minutes. Place in the refrigerator to speed up the process. Spray a long knife with nonstick cooking spray and cut the caramels into ½-inch squares.

Makes **40** Servings

Anyone else going to admit to eating Nutella straight from the jar? This Picky Palate recipe quickly became a reader favorite the day I posted it. Mini marshmallows and Nutella enclosed in buttery, flaky puff pastry produce a dessert that is sure to please. Have the kids help layer the marshmallows over the chocolate. Serve warm or at room temperature dusted with powdered sugar.

Nutella-Mallow Pillow Pockets

2 sheets frozen puff pastry, at room temperature
1 cup Nutella
1 cup mini marshmallows
1 large egg white
4 tablespoons granulated sugar
¼ cup powdered sugar

1. Preheat the oven to 350°F and line a large baking sheet with parchment paper or a silicone liner.

2. Cut each square of puff pastry into 4 equal-size pieces and place on the prepared baking sheet. Spread 2 tablespoons of the Nutella on each pastry, leaving a ½-inch border around the edges. Top each with 12 to 15 mini marshmallows and fold the pastry over the filling to form a triangle. With a fork, crimp the edges firmly. Add the egg white and 1 tablespoon of water to a small bowl, whisk to combine, then lightly brush over pastries. Sprinkle with granulated sugar. Bake for 22 to 25 minutes, until the pastry turns golden brown. Remove and let cool for 5 minutes, and dust with powdered sugar.

Makes
8
Servings

It's no secret I love playing around with the peanut butter and jelly flavor combination. This simple monkey bread recipe using refrigerated biscuits has been a big hit on Picky Palate. I enjoy baking mine in a cast-iron skillet, but you can also use an 8×8-inch baking dish or a 9-inch cake pan if desired. Make sure to have a tall glass of milk ready when these come out of the oven.

Peanut Butter and Jelly Skillet Monkey Bread

1	can refrigerated biscuits (8 count)
4	tablespoons butter, unsalted, melted
¼	cup granulated sugar
¼	cup creamy peanut butter
½	cup jam or jelly of choice
¼	cup heavy cream
½	cup powdered sugar

1. Preheat the oven to 350°F and spray a 9-inch cast-iron skillet with nonstick cooking spray.

2. Cut each biscuit into fourths. Add the melted butter to a large zip-top bag and add the cut biscuits. Shake the bag to coat the biscuits, then add the sugar to the bag and mix to combine. Pour the coated biscuits into the prepared 9-inch cast-iron skillet.

3. In a microwave-safe bowl, heat the peanut butter in the microwave until liquid-like, about 30 seconds. Do the same with the jelly and drizzle both over the biscuits. Bake for 18 to 22 minutes, until cooked through and golden.

4. Add the heavy cream and powdered sugar to a medium bowl, mixing until combined. Drizzle over the warm biscuits. Serve warm.

Makes
6
Servings

Apples and peanut butter are such a great flavor combination for kids and adults. I created this lovely tart that I shared on Picky Palate with simple everyday ingredients. I love having the boys gather round the counter and help layer the apple slices over the peanut butter. This tart can be prepared in under an hour. Serve warm or at room temperature with a tall glass of milk.

Honeyed Apple–Peanut Butter Tart

1   sheet frozen puff pastry, room temperature

½   cup creamy peanut butter

6   tablespoons honey, warmed, divided

2   apples of choice, sliced thinly

2   tablespoons granulated sugar

¼   cup powdered sugar, for dusting

1. Preheat the oven to 350°F and line a large baking sheet with parchment paper or a silicone liner.

2. Cut the puff pastry into 3 equal-size rectangles and place on the prepared baking sheet. In a microwave-safe bowl, heat the peanut butter in the microwave until liquid-like, about 30 seconds. Add 2 tablespoons of the honey and stir to combine, then spread evenly over the 3 pastry rectangles, leaving a ½-inch border around the edges.

3. Layer the apple slices neatly over the peanut butter. In a microwave-safe bowl, heat 2 tablespoons of the remaining honey in the microwave for 15 seconds, until liquid-like. Drizzle over the apples, sprinkle with the sugar, and bake for 30 to 35 minutes, until the pastry is lightly browned and puffed around the edges. Let cool completely, then drizzle with the remaining 2 tablespoons honey. Dust with the powdered sugar. Serve as whole tarts or cut each tart into fourths.

Makes
4
Servings

One of my favorite things about this dessert is that it is so quick to prepare. There isn't one person who will guess how easy a recipe it is. It will be our little secret. Oreo cookies are ground up for the crust with a delightful cream cheese filling that does not need to be baked, just chilled. The kids love to put all of the Oreo cookies into the food processor and watch them mix until finely ground.

Cookie-Crusted Chocolate Chip Cream Cheese Tart

14	Oreo cookies (1½ cups)
3	tablespoons unsalted butter, melted
16	ounces cream cheese, softened
¾	cup packed light brown sugar
1	tablespoon vanilla extract
1	cup semi-sweet chocolate chips

1. Preheat the oven to 350°F and spray a 9-inch tart pan with nonstick cooking spray.

2. Add the Oreo cookies to a food processor and process until finely ground. Add the ground cookies and melted butter to a medium bowl and mix to combine. Press into the bottom of the prepared tart pan. Bake for 10 minutes, remove from the oven, and let cool for 15 minutes.

3. Add the cream cheese, brown sugar, and vanilla to the bowl of a stand mixer and beat until well combined. Add the chocolate chips and mix to combine. Pour into the cooled crust and refrigerate for 2 hours, until firm enough to cut into wedges.

Makes
8
Servings

These peanut butter and jelly baby pies are so much fun to prepare. You simply put teaspoonfuls of peanut butter and jelly inside refrigerated pie crust that's been pressed in mini muffin cups. You can create a lattice topping as I do for this recipe, or you can lay a round cut crust on top. Have the kids help sprinkle sugar over the top of each baked pie. These adorable mini pies are the perfect treat to bring to a party or great for an afternoon snack.

Peanut Butter and Jelly Baby Lattice Pies

1	9-inch refrigerated pie crust, at room temperature
½	cup creamy peanut butter
1	tablespoon sugar
½	cup strawberry preserves
1	large egg white
¼	cup sugar crystal sprinkles
2	tablespoons powdered sugar

1. Preheat the oven to 350°F and spray a 12-count mini muffin pan with nonstick cooking spray.

2. Unroll the pie crust onto a lightly floured countertop. With a 2½-inch round cutter, cut circles out of the dough. Press the dough rounds into the prepared muffin pan. Roll the scraps of dough to an even thickness and use a sharp knife to cut ⅛-inch strips for the lattice topping. Set aside.

3. Add the peanut butter and sugar to a medium bowl and mix to combine. With a small cookie scoop or teaspoon, drop a heaping teaspoon into each mini pie crust. Do the same with the jam. Use the pie strips to form the lattice top. Cut the excess dough from the edges of the pies. Add the egg white and 1 teaspoon of water to a small bowl, whisk to combine, and brush over the tops of the pies. Sprinkle with the sugar crystal sprinkles and bake for 25 to 30 minutes, until golden brown.

4. Remove from the oven and with the tip of a knife, loosen the edges where jam has oozed out. Let the pies cool for 5 minutes before removing from pan. Dust with powdered sugar and serve.

Makes
12
Servings

Carrot cake is one of life's sweetest pleasures. It makes appearances in my family quite often. I love preparing this recipe in a bread pan with a thick layer of cream cheese frosting. There is nothing better, in my opinion. This simple recipe will put smiles on everyone's face. Enjoy with a tall glass of milk.

Carrot Cake Loaf with Thick Cream Cheese Frosting

1¼	cups (2½ sticks) unsalted butter, softened, divided
1¼	cups granulated sugar
2	large eggs
¾	cup buttermilk
2	cups shredded carrots
2¼	cups all-purpose flour
2	teaspoons baking powder
1	teaspoon baking soda
1½	teaspoons ground cinnamon
½	teaspoon kosher salt
4	ounces cream cheese, softened
1½	cups powdered sugar

1. Preheat the oven to 350°F and spray a 9×5×2¾-inch bread pan with nonstick cooking spray.

2. Add 2 sticks of the butter and the sugar to the bowl of a stand mixer and beat until well combined. Add the eggs, one at a time, then slowly add the buttermilk and carrots, beating until well combined.

3. Add the flour, baking powder, baking soda, cinnamon, and salt to a large bowl and mix to combine. Slowly add to the wet ingredients and mix until just combined. Pour into the prepared pan and bake for 50 to 60 minutes, until cooked through. Let cool completely.

4. Add the cream cheese and the remaining ½ stick butter to the bowl of a stand mixer and beat on medium speed until smooth. Slowly add the powdered sugar, beating until well combined. Spread the frosting on top of the cooled bread, slice, and serve.

Makes **10** Servings

Chapter 10

Bake Sale and Beyond

One of my favorite desserts to order at restaurants is the giant pizza cookie served in a hot cast-iron skillet topped with soft vanilla ice cream that melts faster than you can pick up your spoon. I developed a buttery, crisp chocolate chip cookie recipe that tastes just like the ones I have such fond memories of. You can bake your cookie dough in a cake pan or a muffin tin if you do not have a cast-iron skillet. Grab a handful of spoons and share this dessert with your dearest friends and family.

Skillet Chocolate Chip Cookie

10	tablespoons unsalted butter, softened, divided
½	cup granulated sugar
½	cup packed light brown sugar
1	large egg
2	teaspoons vanilla extract
1¼	cups all-purpose flour
½	teaspoon baking soda
½	teaspoon kosher salt
1	cup semi-sweet chocolate chips
	Vanilla ice cream

1. Preheat the oven to 350°F and grease the bottom and sides of a 9-inch cast-iron skillet with 2 tablespoons of the butter.

2. Add the remaining 8 tablespoons of butter and the sugars to the bowl of a stand mixer and beat until light and fluffy. Add the egg and vanilla, beating until well combined.

3. Add the flour, baking soda, and salt to a large bowl and mix to combine. Add the dry ingredients to the wet ingredients, mixing on low. Add the chocolate chips and mix on low until just combined. Press the cookie dough into the prepared skillet and bake for 20 to 25 minutes, until the edges are crisp and the cookie is golden and cooked through. Remove from oven. Serve warm topped with vanilla ice cream.

Makes
8
Servings

I liken this cookie to an ice cream I get often at an ice cream shop we visit regularly. I can't decide which I like better, the ice cream or this soft, chocolaty, gooey cookie. Adding a box of instant chocolate pudding mix right into my cookie dough makes for a soft and chewy texture. Have the kids help add the marshmallows straight to the mix or press them right on top before baking.

Chocolate Peanut Butter and Marshmallow Pudding Cookies

8	ounces (2 sticks) unsalted butter, softened
½	cup granulated sugar
½	cup packed light brown sugar
2	large eggs
1	tablespoon vanilla extract
2¼	cups all-purpose flour
1	teaspoon baking soda
½	teaspoon kosher salt
1	4-ounce box instant chocolate pudding mix
1	10-ounce bag peanut butter chips
1½	cups mini marshmallows

1. Preheat the oven to 350°F and line a large baking sheet with parchment paper or a silicone liner.

2. Add the butter and sugars to the bowl of a stand mixer and beat until light and fluffy. Add the eggs and vanilla, beating until well combined.

3. Add the flour, baking soda, and salt to a large bowl and stir to combine. Slowly add the dry ingredients to the wet ingredients, then add the chocolate pudding mix, peanut butter chips, and marshmallows, beating until just combined.

4. With a medium cookie scoop, place the dough onto the prepared baking sheet, 1 inch apart, and bake for 10 to 12 minutes, until the edges begin to turn golden brown. Let cool for 10 minutes before transferring to cooling rack.

Makes
3
Dozen
Cookies

I remember playing in the kitchen creating this recipe, being so curious as to how they'd turn out with so few ingredients. This is now one of my "go to" cookie recipes when I want a sweet indulgence or am in need of a plate of cookies for a friend when time is short. This is a great recipe to have the kids help measure and stir the ingredients. With only four ingredients, you can have homemade cookies prepared in under 30 minutes.

Browned Butter–Peanut Butter Cookies

4	tablespoons (½ stick) unsalted butter
¾	cup granulated sugar
1	large egg
1	cup creamy peanut butter

1. Preheat the oven to 350°F and line a large baking sheet with parchment paper or a silicone liner.

2. Cut the butter into fourths, and melt in a small saucepan over medium heat, whisking frequently; the butter will bubble, have a nutty aroma, start to brown, and brown specks will form at the bottom of the pan in 2 to 4 minutes. Remove and let cool for 10 minutes.

3. Add the sugar and egg to a medium bowl and mix to combine. Slowly add the browned butter and stir to combine. Add the peanut butter, stirring, until well combined.

4. Scoop 2 tablespoons of the dough onto the prepared baking sheet, about 1 inch apart. Bake for 13 to 15 minutes, until crisp on the outside. Remove and let cool for 10 minutes on the baking sheet before transferring to a cooling rack.

Makes
1½
Dozen
Cookies

When I developed this recipe and shared it on Picky Palate, I had no idea what a cookie sensation they would become. Foodies all over the country were making my cookies and posting them all over the web; it was great. I remember visiting my family in Arizona during our Christmas vacation, when I was rummaging through my mom's cupboard. I saw a bag of Double Stuf Oreos and I quickly pulled my mom into the kitchen so we could get to work on the monster-size stuffed cookie I had in mind. The reactions you get when you cut open these cookies are priceless.

Oreo-Stuffed Chocolate Chip Cookies

8	ounces (2 sticks) unsalted butter, softened
¾	cup packed light brown sugar
1	cup granulated sugar
2	large eggs
1	tablespoon vanilla extract
3½	cups all-purpose flour
1	teaspoon kosher salt
1	teaspoon baking soda
1	10-ounce bag semi-sweet chocolate chips
1	1 pound 2 ounce bag Double Stuf Oreo Cookies

1. Preheat the oven to 350°F and line a large baking sheet with parchment paper or a silicone liner.

2. Add the butter and sugars to the bowl of a stand mixer, beating until light and fluffy. Add the eggs and vanilla, beating until well combined.

3. Add the flour, salt, and baking soda to a large bowl and stir to combine. Slowly add the dry ingredients to the wet ingredients, then add the chocolate chips, beating until just combined. With a large cookie scoop, take one scoop of cookie dough and place it on top of an Oreo cookie. Take another scoop of dough and place it on the bottom of the Oreo cookie. Seal the edges together by pressing and cupping the dough in hand until the Oreo cookie is completely enclosed and is in the shape of a patty. Repeat with the remaining dough and cookies.

4. Place the stuffed cookies onto a prepared baking sheet, 1 inch apart, and bake for 11 to 15 minutes, until the cookies are cooked through. Let cool for 5 minutes before transferring to cooling rack.

Makes 18–24 Cookies

There's nothing I enjoy more than getting in the kitchen and whipping up a batch of cookies with my boys. They sit at the counter and help add all of the ingredients to the mixer, sneaking bites of dough along the way. These cookies are packed with dried blueberries, white chocolate, and oatmeal. Enjoy with a tall glass of milk.

Blueberry–White Chocolate Oatmeal Cookies

8	ounces (2 sticks) unsalted butter, softened
¾	cup granulated sugar
1	cup packed light brown sugar
2	large eggs
1½	tablespoons vanilla extract
2½	cups all-purpose flour
2½	cups rolled oats
1	teaspoon baking soda
1	teaspoon kosher salt
1½	cups dried blueberries
1	cup white chocolate chips

1. Preheat the oven to 350°F and line a large baking sheet with parchment paper or a silicone liner.

2. Add the butter and sugars to the bowl of a stand mixer and beat until light and fluffy. Add the eggs and vanilla, beating until well combined.

3. Add the flour, oats, baking soda, and salt to a large bowl and stir to combine. Slowly add the dry ingredients to the wet ingredients, then the blueberries and white chocolate chips, beating until just combined.

4. With a medium cookie scoop, place the dough onto the prepared baking sheet 1 inch apart, and bake for 9 to 11 minutes, until the edges are just turning golden brown. Let cool for 5 minutes before transferring to a cooling rack.

Makes **4** Dozen Cookies

It's no secret on Picky Palate that I love creating cookies. I remember browsing through the baking aisle at the grocery store when I picked up a box of almond paste, wondering what I could do with it. I had never used it in a recipe before, but immediately thought it would be perfect to add in chocolate chip cookies. Sure enough, it was. Have the kids sit at the counter and help add the ingredients to the mixer. The almond paste gives a nice chewy texture with a perfect hint of almond.

Almond Lovers' Chocolate Chip Cookies

8	ounces (2 sticks) unsalted butter, softened
¾	cup granulated sugar
¾	cup packed light brown sugar
3	ounces pure almond paste
2	large eggs
1	tablespoon vanilla extract
2½	cups all-purpose flour
1	teaspoon baking soda
½	teaspoon kosher salt
1	12-ounce bag semi-sweet chocolate chips
¾	cup chopped almonds

1. Preheat the oven to 350°F and line a large baking sheet with parchment paper or a silicone liner.

2. Add the butter and sugars to the bowl of a stand mixer, beating until light and fluffy. Add the almond paste in pieces, beating until well combined. Add the eggs and vanilla, beating until well combined.

3. Add the flour, baking soda, and salt to a large bowl and stir to combine. Slowly add the dry ingredients to the wet ingredients, then the chocolate chips and almonds, beating until just combined.

4. With a medium cookie scoop, place the dough onto the prepared baking sheet 1 inch apart and bake for 10 to 12 minutes, until the edges just start to turn golden brown. Let cool for 5 minutes before transferring to a cooling rack.

Makes 3 Dozen Cookies

What is it about the s'mores ingredients that makes such fun recipes? I have enjoyed playing around with this combination of flavors on Picky Palate. The marshmallows bake up nice and gooey alongside the graham cracker pieces and chocolate bar rectangles. The kids have a blast adding the s'mores pieces to the dough before they bake. This simple cake-mix cookie will leave you wishing you had made a double batch.

Chocolate Cake S'mores Cookies

1	18.25-ounce box devil's food cake mix
2	large eggs
¼	cup packed light brown sugar
8	tablespoons (1 stick) unsalted butter, melted
3	1.55-ounce Hershey's chocolate bars, cut into rectangles
1½	cups mini marshmallows
1½	cups roughly chopped graham crackers

1. Preheat the oven to 350°F and line a large baking sheet with parchment paper or a silicone liner.

2. Add the cake mix, eggs, brown sugar, and butter to a large bowl and mix until combined. With a medium cookie scoop, place the dough onto the prepared baking sheet, 1 inch apart. Press the cookies to flatten to about ½ inch thick. Press a chocolate bar piece, 2 marshmallows and 2 graham cracker pieces on top of the flattened cookie dough. Bake for 11 to 13 minutes, until cooked through. Let cool for 5 minutes before transferring to a cooling rack.

Makes
3
Dozen
Cookies

I remember talking to my sister a few years ago, when she went on and on about how she was using coconut oil in about everything from frying eggs to even eating it by the spoonfuls for its health benefits. I was intrigued, to say the least. It turns out that it's delicious as a substitute for butter in cookies. Surprisingly, you don't get a strong coconut taste in your cookies from the oil. We are huge cinnamon chip fans in my family, but if you can't find them at your grocery store, simply substitute with extra chocolate chips.

Cinnamon and White Chocolate Coconut-Oat Chippers

1	cup virgin coconut oil, softened
¾	cup granulated sugar
¾	cup packed light brown sugar
2	large eggs
1	teaspoon vanilla extract
2¼	cups all-purpose flour
1¼	cups rolled oats
1	teaspoon baking soda
¾	teaspoon kosher salt
1½	cups shredded sweetened coconut
1½	cups cinnamon chips
1½	cups white chocolate chips

1. Preheat the oven to 375°F and line a large baking sheet with parchment paper or a silicone liner.

2. Add the oil and sugars to a stand mixer and beat until well combined. Add the eggs and vanilla, beating until well combined.

3. Add the flour, oats, baking soda, and salt to a large bowl and stir to combine. Slowly add the dry ingredients to the wet ingredients, then the coconut, cinnamon chips, and white chocolate chips, beating until just combined.

4. With a medium cookie scoop, place the dough onto the prepared baking sheet 1 inch apart and bake for 9 to 11 minutes, until the edges just start to turn golden brown. Let cool for 5 minutes before transferring to a cooling rack.

Makes
3
Dozen
Cookies

Homemade brownies can be very tricky. I was determined to create a recipe exactly how I like my brownies . . . fudgy, dense, and gooey. I added peanut butter and mini marshmallows to help achieve my perfect brownie. Omit the peanut butter and marshmallows for a plain, thick brownie if desired. Try stuffing with your favorite cookie, candy bar, or preserves as well. The kids love being in charge of layering the marshmallows and drizzling the peanut butter. Serve with a glass of milk and a side of ice cream.

Peanut Butter–Marshmallow Fudgy Brownies

8	tablespoons (1 stick) unsalted butter
2	cups semi-sweet chocolate chips
1	cup all-purpose flour
½	cup granulated sugar
½	cup packed light brown sugar
½	teaspoon kosher salt
2	large eggs plus 1 egg yolk
2	tablespoons canola or vegetable oil
1	cup mini marshmallows
¼	cup creamy peanut butter

1. Preheat the oven to 350°F and line an 8×8-inch baking dish with foil and spray with nonstick cooking spray.

2. Melt the butter in a medium saucepan over medium heat, stirring continuously. Add the chocolate chips, stirring, until melted. Remove from the heat.

3. Add the flour, sugars, and salt to a large bowl and stir to combine. Slowly add the melted chocolate mixture, eggs plus egg yolk, and oil, stirring until well combined. Transfer half of the brownie mixture to the prepared baking dish and top with the marshmallows. In a microwave-safe bowl, heat the peanut butter in the microwave until liquid-like, about 30 seconds. Pour over the marshmallow layer, then top with the remaining brownie batter. The batter is thick and does not need to be perfectly spread over the peanut butter and marshmallow layers.

4. Bake for 30 to 35 minutes, until cooked through. Let cool completely, remove from the pan, and cut into bars.

Makes
9–12
Brownies

This over-the-top brownie recipe has been a Picky Palate favorite for quite some time now. Jazzing up brownie mixes is something I love to do. Adding a big scoop of your favorite ice cream to this mix bakes up a rich, decadent treat that is fun to share with the whole family. Play around with different flavors of ice cream for a new batch of brownies each time.

Ice Cream Sundae Brownies

1	18.3-ounce box brownie mix
2	large eggs
½	cup vegetable oil
½	cup ice cream of choice, slightly softened
1½	cups semi-sweet chocolate chips
¼	cup prepared hot fudge topping, chilled

1. Preheat the oven to 350°F and line a 9×13-inch baking dish with foil and spray with nonstick cooking spray.

2. Add the brownie mix, eggs, and oil to a large bowl and mix until combined. *Do not add the water as directed on the box.* Add the ice cream (slightly softened), chocolate chips, and hot fudge and stir to combine.

3. Pour the brownie batter into the prepared baking dish and bake for 40 to 50 minutes, until a toothpick comes out nearly clean from the center. Let cool completely, remove from the baking dish, cut into squares, and serve.

Makes 12 Brownies

This is another Picky Palate favorite brownie recipe that is simple to prepare and is stuffed with all of those delicious s'mores ingredients—graham crackers, chocolate, and marshmallows. With so few ingredients, these brownies will be on your table in no time at all. This is a great recipe to have the kids help layer the s'mores ingredients over the brownies. Make sure you have a tall glass of milk ready when serving.

S'mores Stuffed Brownies

1	18.3-ounce box brownie mix
4½	sheets graham crackers
3½	1.55-ounce Hershey's chocolate bars
16	large marshmallows

1. Preheat the oven to 350°F and line an 8×8-inch baking pan with foil and spray with nonstick cooking spray.

2. Prepare the brownie mix according to the package directions. Pour half of the brownie batter into the prepared baking pan. Layer the graham crackers, chocolate, and marshmallows on top. Pour the remaining brownie batter over the marshmallows.

3. Bake for 40 to 45 minutes, until a toothpick comes out nearly clean from the center. Let cool completely, remove the foil from the baking dish, cut into squares, and serve.

Makes
12
Brownies

I'll never forget my first jar of gourmet butterscotch peanut butter from Spread Restaurant in San Diego. I could not believe the incredible peanut butter combinations that were available at this restaurant. I was in awe. The second I got home, I went to work in my kitchen like a mad scientist, experimenting with butterscotch and peanut butter. These bars are now one of my "go to" desserts and take just minutes to prepare. Have the kids help measure out the ingredients and help stir. Serve chilled with a tall glass of milk.

No-Bake Chocolate–Peanut Butter–Butterscotch Bars

2	cups butterscotch chips
4	tablespoons (½ stick) unsalted butter, softened, divided
2	cups creamy peanut butter
1	cup powdered sugar
1	12-ounce bag semi-sweet chocolate chips
¼	cup heavy cream

1. Line an 8×8-inch baking pan with foil and spray with nonstick cooking spray.

2. Add the butterscotch chips and 2 tablespoons of the butter to the bowl of a double boiler to melt. Stir until melted; the mixture will have the consistency of peanut butter. Remove from the heat. Add the peanut butter and melted butterscotch chips to a large bowl and mix to combine. Add the powdered sugar, and stir until smooth. Transfer the peanut butter mixture to the prepared baking pan, spreading evenly.

3. Wash and dry the bowl of the double boiler and add the chocolate chips and the remaining 2 tablespoons butter to melt. Stir until melted, then add the heavy cream, stirring, until smooth. Pour over the peanut butter layer in the pan, spreading evenly.

4. Refrigerate for 1 hour or until firm. Lift the foil edges to remove from the pan and cut into squares. Serve chilled or at room temperature.

Makes
9
Large Bars

This is by far a Picky Palate favorite recipe. It's great to have on hand when you need dessert and are short on time. It's perfect as an after-school snack, and great for bake sales. The kids love to grind the Oreo cookies in the food processor and help mix the marshmallows. With only 3 ingredients, you'll only need about 20 minutes from start to finish, and you'll have irresistible chewy cookie bars that disappear about as fast as you get them to the table.

No-Bake Chewy Cookies and Cream Bars

1	16-ounce package of Oreo cookies
32	large marshmallows
4	tablespoons (½ stick) butter

1. Line an 8×8-inch baking dish with foil and spray with nonstick cooking spray.

2. Add the Oreos to a food processor and pulse until coarsely ground. Transfer to a large mixing bowl.

3. In a microwave-safe bowl, heat the marshmallows and butter in the microwave until puffed, 1½ to 2 minutes. Add to the ground Oreos, quickly stir to combine, then transfer to the prepared baking dish, pressing evenly. Let sit for 10 minutes on the countertop to firm up. Lift the foil edges to remove from the pan and cut into squares.

Makes
9
Large Bars

Extras

This is a collection of sauces, dressings, frostings, and more that can be whipped up in no time.

This is a great sauce that goes beautifully over pasta, chicken, beef, or seafood. Not only is it tasty, it also only takes about 10 minutes to prepare.

Fire-Roasted Tomato Cream Sauce

2	14-ounce cans Muir Glen Fire-Roasted Diced Tomatoes
½	cup heavy cream
¼	teaspoon kosher salt
¼	teaspoon freshly ground black pepper
¼	teaspoon garlic salt

Add the tomatoes to a food processor and pulse until nearly smooth. Transfer to a large saucepan over medium-low heat. Add the heavy cream, salt, pepper, and garlic salt and cook, stirring, for 5 minutes. Serve over pasta or rice. Store in an airtight container in the refrigerator for 3 to 5 days.

This peanut sauce is the perfect addition to chicken and pasta. It's creamy, quick to prepare, and absolutely delicious.

Peanut-Ginger Sauce

½	cup creamy peanut butter
¼	cup reduced-sodium soy sauce
2	tablespoons packed light brown sugar
1½	tablespoons grated fresh ginger
1	tablespoon minced garlic
1	tablespoon rice wine vinegar

Add the peanut butter, soy sauce, brown sugar, ginger, garlic, and vinegar to a blender and blend until smooth. Slowly add 1 cup of hot water, blending until smooth. Serve over chicken or pasta. Store in an airtight container in the refrigerator for 7 to 10 days.

It's so nice to make your own BBQ sauce. You'll be surprised at how easy it is to prepare. Enjoy this sauce over chicken, beef, or pork, or use as a dip.

Homemade BBQ Sauce

1½	cups ketchup
¼	cup Worcestershire sauce
¼	cup packed light brown sugar
3	tablespoons yellow mustard
2	tablespoons vinegar
1½	tablespoons fresh lemon juice
1	teaspoon freshly ground black pepper
¼	teaspoon kosher salt

Add the ketchup, Worcestershire sauce, brown sugar, mustard, vinegar, lemon juice, pepper, and salt to a medium saucepan over medium-low heat and stir to combine. Cook, stirring, for 5 minutes. Serve with chicken, beef, or pork. Store in an airtight container in the refrigerator for 7 to 10 days.

This zesty sauce is great over tacos, chicken, rice, and even salad.

Cilantro Cream Sauce

½	cup sour cream
½	cup chopped fresh cilantro leaves
½	teaspoon lime juice
¼	teaspoon kosher salt
¼	teaspoon freshly ground black pepper
¼	teaspoon hot sauce, like Tabasco

Add the sour cream, cilantro, lime juice, salt, pepper, and hot sauce to a medium bowl and stir to combine. Serve in burritos, over tacos, or as a dip. Store in an airtight container in the refrigerator for 7 to 10 days.

It's quite rewarding to have a beautiful homemade pasta sauce to pour over your favorite pasta or chicken. Once your vegetables are chopped, this sauce can be done in about 15 minutes.

Homemade Vegetable Pasta Sauce

2	tablespoons extra-virgin olive oil
1	cup finely chopped white onion
1	cup chopped zucchini
1	cup chopped fresh spinach leaves
¼	cup finely chopped mini sweet peppers
1	tablespoon minced garlic
1	28-ounce can crushed tomatoes
¼	cup chopped fresh basil leaves
¾	teaspoon kosher salt
¼	teaspoon freshly ground black pepper
¼	teaspoon garlic salt
¼	teaspoon Italian seasoning
½	teaspoon granulated sugar

Heat the olive oil in a Dutch oven or large pot over medium heat. Add the onion, zucchini, spinach, and sweet peppers and cook, stirring, until tender, 8 to 10 minutes. Add the garlic and cook, stirring, for 1 minute. Add the crushed tomatoes, basil, salt, pepper, garlic salt, Italian seasoning, and sugar, reduce the heat to low, and let simmer for at least 15 minutes. Serve over your favorite cooked pasta or chicken dishes. Store in an airtight container in the refrigerator for 7 to 10 days.

This enchilada sauce makes some of the best Mexican-style dinners. Enchiladas, burritos, tacos, rice, you name it, this sauce makes a great addition. I place any leftover sauce in zip-top bags and freeze to use for another dinner.

Homemade Red Enchilada Sauce

2	tablespoons extra-virgin olive oil
2	cups finely chopped white onion
6	cloves garlic
1	28-ounce can crushed or diced tomatoes
1	cup reduced-sodium chicken broth
¼	cup cornmeal
¼	cup chili powder
2	tablespoons ground cumin
1	tablespoon packed light brown sugar
½	tablespoon smoked paprika
¾	teaspoon kosher salt
¼	teaspoon freshly ground black pepper

Add the olive oil in a Dutch oven or large pot over medium heat. Add the onion and garlic and cook, stirring, until tender, about 5 minutes. Add the tomatoes, chicken broth, cornmeal, chili powder, cumin, brown sugar, paprika, salt, and pepper and stir to combine. Reduce the heat to low and simmer for 15 minutes. In batches, transfer the sauce into a blender and blend until smooth. Return to the pot to simmer for at least 15 minutes. Serve over your favorite Mexican-style meal. Store in an airtight container in the refrigerator for 7 to 10 days.

We are a family that dips nearly everything in ranch dressing, from pizza to chicken fingers to quesadillas, so it was a priority for me to make a healthier, homemade version for my family. I have tested this recipe on my kids and husband, and it passed the test. Serve with salad, or whatever your family likes.

Homemade Ranch Dressing

¾	cup buttermilk
½	cup plain Greek yogurt
½	cup mayonnaise
¼	cup finely chopped white onion
1	tablespoon freshly grated Parmesan cheese
1	tablespoon chopped fresh parsley leaves
2	teaspoons white vinegar
1	teaspoon dried thyme
½	teaspoon kosher salt
¼	teaspoon freshly ground black pepper
¼	teaspoon garlic salt

Add all ingredients to a blender and blend until smooth and combined, about 30 seconds. Store in an airtight container in the refrigerator for up to 2 weeks.

Sometimes it's nice to whisk a fresh and simple dressing to go over your salad greens. This is one of my favorites in a pinch.

Simple Lemon Dressing

½	cup extra-virgin olive oil
2	tablespoons fresh lemon juice
½	teaspoon kosher salt
½	teaspoon granulated sugar
¼	teaspoon freshly ground black pepper

Add the olive oil, lemon juice, salt, sugar, and pepper to a medium bowl and whisk until emulsified and combined. Drizzle over salads. Store in an airtight container in the refrigerator for 7 to 10 days.

This simple dry rub makes your chicken, beef, pork, or even seafood full of sweet and smoky flavor. It's one of my favorites.

Sweet and Smoky Dry Rub

¼	cup packed light brown sugar
1	teaspoon smoked paprika
1	teaspoon kosher salt
½	teaspoon freshly ground black pepper
¼	teaspoon garlic salt
¼	teaspoon ground cumin

Add the brown sugar, paprika, salt, pepper, garlic salt, and cumin to a small bowl and stir to combine. Rub over chicken, beef, or pork. Store in an airtight container for 3 months.

There really is nothing like a homemade pie crust. I've developed a very simple one that makes the most delicious pies, both sweet and savory.

Homemade Pie Crust

2¾	cups all-purpose flour
3	tablespoons granulated sugar
1	teaspoon kosher salt
8	ounces (2 sticks) cold unsalted butter, cubed
½	cup ice water

Add the flour, sugar, and salt to a food processor. Pulse to combine. Add the butter and pulse until the mixture is the size of small peas. With the food processor running, slowly add the ice water until combined. Transfer the dough to a lightly floured countertop, kneading a couple of times to combine. Divide the dough in half, flatten slightly, and wrap tightly with plastic wrap. Refrigerate for at least 2 to 3 hours before using. Store the dough wrapped in plastic wrap for 1 week in the refrigerator or 2 months in the freezer.

Cream cheese frosting might just be my favorite frosting ever. It's perfect for chocolate, yellow, and carrot cake. This recipe is enough for roughly 24 cupcakes. I would double it for a double-layer 9-inch cake.

Cream Cheese Frosting

1	8-ounce package cream cheese, softened
8	tablespoons (1 stick) unsalted butter, softened
3	cups powdered sugar

Add the cream cheese and butter to the bowl of a stand mixer, beating on medium speed until smooth. Slowly add the powdered sugar, beating until well combined. Spread over cupcakes or cakes. Store in an airtight container in the refrigerator for 7 to 10 days.

I have to have chocolate frosting along with my cream cheese frosting, and I have found this simple recipe is my favorite. I enjoy it on chocolate or yellow cupcakes and cakes. This recipe is enough for roughly 24 cupcakes.

Chocolate-Buttercream Frosting

1	8-ounce package cream cheese, softened
8	tablespoons (1 stick) unsalted butter, softened
1	cup semi-sweet chocolate chips
3½	cups powdered sugar
¼	cup cocoa powder

Add the cream cheese and butter to the bowl of a stand mixer, beating until well combined. In a microwave-safe bowl, melt the chocolate chips in the microwave in 30-second intervals, stirring until smooth. Slowly add the melted chocolate to the mixer, beating until well combined. Slowly add the powdered sugar and cocoa powder, mixing until well combined. Spread over cupcakes or cakes. Store in an airtight container in the refrigerator for 7 to 10 days.

This simple caramel syrup is delicious over pancakes, waffles, or even ice cream. Chances are you will have these ingredients on hand to whip up any time you'd like.

Caramel Syrup

1	cup packed light brown sugar
¼	teaspoon kosher salt
4	tablespoons (½ stick) unsalted butter
¼	cup heavy cream
¼	cup sour cream

Combine the brown sugar, salt, and 2 tablespoons of water in a small saucepan over medium heat. Stir until bubbly and smooth, about 5 minutes. Add the butter, stirring until melted, then add the heavy cream and sour cream, stirring, until well combined. Reduce the heat to low until ready to serve. Store in an airtight container in the refrigerator for 3 to 5 days.

This is the pancake syrup my kids refer to as the "candy syrup." It is downright sinful and makes those everyday pancakes taste like a million bucks.

Homemade Buttermilk Syrup

8	tablespoons (1 stick) unsalted butter
½	cup granulated sugar
½	cup buttermilk
½	teaspoon baking soda
½	teaspoon vanilla extract

Add the butter, sugar, and buttermilk to a medium saucepan over medium heat, stirring until melted. Once the syrup starts to boil, add the baking soda and vanilla and stir to combine. When the syrup starts to foam, remove from the heat and transfer to serving dish. Drizzle over pancakes. This syrup is best used the same day.

Ice cream topping is much simpler to prepare than you might think. With just a few basic ingredients, you will have a sauce that tastes much better than the ones you buy in the stores.

Salted Caramel Sauce

1	cup granulated sugar
8	tablespoons (1 stick) unsalted butter, cut into ¼-inch cubes
½	teaspoon sea salt
½	cup heavy cream

Add the sugar and ¼ cup of water to a medium saucepan over medium heat. Swirl and stir until the sugar is dissolved. Continue boiling without stirring, just occasionally swirling the pan until the syrup turns deep golden brown. Reduce the heat to low, add the butter pieces, sea salt, and heavy cream and stir to combine. The mixture will boil violently; keep stirring, until combined. Serve over ice cream, or transfer to an airtight container and refrigerate until ready to use, 7 to 10 days. Reheat in the microwave for 60 seconds, or until melted.

This simple hot fudge recipe can be prepared in about 5 minutes and is much better than the store-bought ones.

Simple Hot Fudge Sauce

1	14-ounce can sweetened condensed milk
1	cup semi-sweet chocolate chips

Add the sweetened condensed milk to a medium saucepan over medium heat and cook, stirring constantly, until hot, about 3 minutes. Stir in the chocolate chips until melted and smooth. Serve over ice cream, or transfer to an airtight container and refrigerate until ready to use, 7 to 10 days. Reheat in the microwave for 60 seconds, or until melted.

Index

Pages with photos are in italics.